GW00390997

Don't Be Afraid to Create

Keelan LaForge

ISBN: 9798373818094

Printed in Belfast, United Kingdom.

Publisher – Independently Published

Cover Credit – james@goonwrite.com

<u>Dedication</u>

To anyone that has never felt good enough in creativity or in life, you have always been great at both.

Contents

Chapter One – Self-Doubt

People are always telling me they have no creativity in them. I know that's a falsehood. I don't know why being near someone that practises creativity automatically makes us doubt our own. Everyone is creative. People tell me they don't have a creative bone in their body because they can't draw a picture, or write a story, or sew on a button. But those aren't the bounds of creativity.

I used to believe that I wasn't creative either. I didn't think I could come up with any good ideas. I thought about people that fashioned sea creatures out of toilet roll tubes and pipe cleaners and I felt inadequate. Those ideas didn't immediately spring to my mind. Maybe that just wasn't my area; the area in which my creativity thrived. I thought that in order to be creative that you had to be able to draw lifelike pictures straight out of your head. You couldn't have a reference point from which to work. But now I know that isn't true. I have spoken to so many artists and creatives that take elements of their artwork from other sources. It might be in the form of creating a collage, copying parts of a drawing and incorporating it into something else, piecing together photographic images to come up with their own story. Does that render their work useless? Does that mean they aren't creative? No. Everything that you create comes from a source of inspiration and no idea stands alone like the world on its first day of creation, being or whatever you want to believe.

I believe we were all born to create. Finding out how to do that for yourself is what connects you to your purpose. Even if it's not for the sake of work or personal gain, the act of creating alone brings you joy and satisfaction. People always tell me they like the idea of being "creative" but they just don't know how to do it. I don't know who it was in history that decided what counted as creative and what didn't, or who began labelling artists "true creatives," and everyone else, frauds. Maybe it has just been a pattern of thinking, passed from one generation to another, like a genetically inherited illness. But sooner or later, someone needs to break it and run against it. It has the dangerous ability to rob us of so much.

When I was little, I remember thinking I was unoriginal and untalented. I don't know where beliefs like that originate from, but I had loud self-critiques constantly playing in my head. When I was in my first year of primary school, I remember a boy that was labelled the "creator" of the class. He was obsessed with dinosaurs and spent all his time drawing them. He was great at creating cartoons. Everyone praised him for his efforts. He never seemed as interested in what we were working on in class as he was in his personal drawings. Maybe he felt like he was an ordained artist from birth. The teachers and his classmates certainly confirmed that belief for him. Maybe that was all that he needed: belief in himself and belief coming from others. I think that is what holds so many of us back – our lack of self-belief and the lack of belief from others around us in our early years. Maybe they are blind to our potential, or maybe we are so inclined towards self-doubt that we never have the opportunity to unlock it.

I always loved creating things, but I didn't count myself as "creative." I couldn't draw clever cartoons and amusing illustrations of prehistoric animals straight from my head, so I thought there was only one "artist of the class." The thing is: there is always an artist of the group, wherever we go in life. It is one person that has been labelled "successful," so there is no room left for the rest of us to try to be. In our society, we are made to feel like there is only room for one talent and the rest of us just become part of the audience.

Why can't we all just take it in turns being members of the audience and let each person have their opportunity to take to the stage in whatever way they feel comfortable doing? Who decided that there could only be one exceptional person per class or per social group?

I don't know where these ideas stem from, but they are lies created to keep us small. I think they should all be broken down so we can all step on to our own stages. There has been one constructed for each of us. And in saying that, I don't mean that we all have to be loud performers, but there is room for us all to occupy whatever space feels natural to us. We should stop letting other people shut us down and dismiss us. Most of the time, they probably don't even consciously realise they are doing it. They've been programmed in the same way that we have.

For example, imagine your grandfather was always told that he was terrible at drawing. He might have had a tyrant of a teacher in the days before the implementation of positive teaching methods. He might have drawn his own sketches and was chastised for being a daydreamer, or maybe he never bothered to draw at all because his first picture was dismissed as no good. Maybe his parents told him that they couldn't draw either and that there just aren't any artists in the family. Maybe they failed to see the other ways in which they were using their creativity in their daily lives. That notion spreads throughout a family like a highly infectious disease and no one stops to question it because they feel they can't disprove it. It travels from one generation to the next, until generations later, you find yourself saying that you can't draw a stick man and that everyone in your family has always been exactly the same. That's the persistent and pervasive pattern of creative slaying that happens in so many of our lives.

Chapter Two – Line Drawings aren't the only Form of Art

I meet so many people who believe that they can't draw. For some reason, not being able to draw is automatically paired with not being able to create. I don't think that anyone "can't draw." Maybe some people don't want to draw, or they have no interest in drawing, but everyone is capable of their own style of drawing. Maybe one person can't draw an accurate portrait of someone, but they can draw patterns, or they can draw cartoons, or motifs or fancy writing. We all have our own way in which we interpret the same task.

There are artists' work I have seen that have no merit in terms of accurately representing whatever they are trying to capture. That doesn't mean that their work isn't "art." Maybe, in a way, it is more artful, because their minds and hands are producing a new perspective on whatever object or scene they are trying to recreate. Everyone sees something different when they look at the same picture, and everyone's taste is different. There is a place in the world for everyone's work, however much the person might hate it themselves. Sometimes the work that you are least proud of speaks the most profoundly to someone else.

People often think that they "can't create" when they don't draw pictures, or when they can't make a "very hungry caterpillar" out of cast- offs they've retrieved from the recycling bin. That just isn't the case. There are a million different ways to create, and we are always doing it, even when it isn't conscious.

I realised this recently when I went trick or treating with my kids. There is so much creativity in the world that is overlooked or that isn't

9

acknowledged as such. When we were walking around and scouting out houses with signs of Halloween celebration displayed around them (hence, a better chance of a plentiful supply of sweets for the kids,) I noticed how many interesting displays there were. People go to real effort now to dress their houses up for Halloween. I love the fun of it and the festivity with which it fills a darker season of the year. Some displays are simple, and others are incredibly elaborate, but it's the creative expression that I value and the community contribution. You don't put lights outside your house for your own benefit; you do it to cheer up someone else. How many people sit in their gardens at night, admiring their fairy lights and decorations from the outside? It's the community-spirited demonstration of joy and humour that I love to see.

At one house, someone had made a stand for their Halloween ornaments out of overturned crates and hessian material. There were carved pumpkins standing all over it and candles and bowls of sweets. When the kids pressed the doorbell, it spoke to them in a spooky voice, and they were delighted by it. Someone put the time and effort into making that and the kids noticed the creativity that went into it, and they appreciated it. It brought a lot of light into their lives on an otherwise dark evening. I don't know what the backgrounds are of those people. Maybe they work in a creative role, or maybe they work in a grey office building, but they still put their creativity to good use for the Halloween holidays. Just because it isn't recognised with a degree or an award or public acknowledgement of their creative skill, it doesn't diminish the act of it and the fact that it brings joy into someone else's day.

I always thought of one of my grandmothers as creative and the other as not so creative. I realise now that that isn't the truth. One of them practised intentional creativity constantly. She always had a new project on the go. She crocheted impressive blankets, she knitted, she made things out of scraps, she collected beautiful stationary and spent a lot of her time using it at her writing desk. You could see her creativity on display everywhere. It was obvious. My other grandmother didn't practise it so confidently. She didn't refer to her actions as creative, but that didn't mean that they weren't.

She used to get us to dress up at Halloween in old frilly dressing gowns she had and recite poetry at the front door to entertain the adults. She had an organ in her underused front room, and I used to go in there and spend hours playing it and working out the sheet music for it. She put together elaborate meals and she was great at throwing a party. She came up with simple games for us to play – like "hide the thimble." (An adult had to hide the thimble and then tell us when we were getting hotter or colder as we searched for it.) Her salads were like works of art. We always made fun of her for saying "in the Summer, all you want is a wee salad," because her salads contained more components than her New Year's dinners did. If we went for a picnic, she put so much effort into preparing the food. She'd cook a ham especially for the occasion and fill sandwiches with large slices of it. I can still taste her roast potatoes twenty years since I last had one of them. She was an excellent cook, and she could feed a country without seeming to break into a sweat. Just because someone doesn't call themselves "creative," it doesn't mean that they aren't. You don't have to self-identify as something or let someone else label you as that thing for it to be true. You don't need to get permission to be something you have always naturally been. We don't seek for someone to call us human in order to begin accepting ourselves as such.

Sometimes, it feels like there is a locked room filled with artists and you can only gain access to it if you're a "legitimate" artist. But who is to say that one person is a true artist because they have all the qualifications to back it up, but that someone that sits at home, making embroidery isn't an artist in their own right too? It feels like there is a competition taking place to see who can get the top spot, as if there are limited places, but there aren't. I don't know who created the boundaries around this limited artistic space, but I think we can take it upon ourselves to knock them down. We should create what we feel the desire to create without worrying what other people will think – and without dismissing our own ideas as "silly."

Even if you don't consider yourself to be a "creative" person, you are probably still creating in some form each and every day. Maybe you are good at decorating or organising and you create a pleasant home for yourself, maybe you're always creating in the kitchen, maybe you create stories to entertain other people. Even if they are factual events, you are still proffering them in a creative way – adding your own spin to each one or reconstructing the anecdote to make it as amusing as possible. Maybe you create elaborate Christmas Eve boxes for your kids, or you sit down and draw with your child, or make up a bedtime story. Maybe you create a good atmosphere with music, lights and good food. Maybe you create a lovely garden. Maybe you gift wrap beautifully. Maybe you make your car gleam. The options are interminable. Creativity isn't just completing an impressive portrait, or a watercolour painting that captures the true dimensions of a scene. It can be something much looser than that and freer – it's just putting something of your own into the world (even if it's in your home world) and running with an idea, however small, when it pops into your head.

Chapter Three - Your Ideas Aren't Stupid

Everyone has ideas. That's what happens when you spend your whole life thinking. You might be inspired by something you see and have the idea to do it yourself. Maybe you have valuable ideas, but you just lack the confidence to carry them through and make them into physical things. That isn't your fault. There is a lot of conditioning that takes place in our society. From a young age, kids are told what they thrive at and what they shouldn't waste time doing. It becomes a belief of ours – passed to us from one limited perspective and we wear it like it was a personal decision. It wasn't.

For a long time, I had no confidence in my ideas. In fact, I still don't – I have just learnt how to push through the self-doubt and put my work out there anyway. That doesn't mean it attracts a crowd, or that it sells out – but the act of putting it out there gives me a sense of completion to whatever project I've been working on. I still get loud negative voices in my head, telling me how useless my ideas are or how futile it is going to the bother of communicating them to the world, but my desire to do it is stronger than the self-doubt. Sometimes you have to just tell your self-doubt to shut up and to stop limiting you.

What if everyone dismissed every idea they'd ever had as "stupid?" We would have missed out on so much amazing art, as well as technological advances and essential items we use every day. I don't believe that any idea is inherently "bad" and allowing yourself to brainstorm and acknowledge your ideas as valuable enables you to select the ones you really want to run with. Even if you share a half-formed idea, someone else might be inspired to take action to complete it or come up with the missing link you needed to make it work.

This is why I have never understood how Art is graded in school. It's hard to work out how you'd come up with a standardised system for something so intangible. Or does it just depend on the taste of the invigilator? I had an art teacher that loved my paintings in school. She talked about them constantly, telling me that I would get an A* in GCSE Art. At the end of the year, an external examiner came in to mark our work. I was awarded a B for my work. It really discouraged me at the time, and I gave up art, but one person's opinion on your work shouldn't hold you back. Every artist has fans of their work and people that just don't "get it." It's not a sign of failure; it's a difference in personal taste. If everyone liked the same stuff, the world would be extremely boring, and everything would always be sold out. For every person that hates your ideas, there will be many more that adore them.

Some people might think they don't have ideas, but maybe they just aren't acting on them. Fleeting thoughts that you grab hold of can become concrete ideas you later see sitting in front of you. You just have to take the time to notice them and not write them off as "useless."

Sometimes I meet people that are otherwise confident, but they lack creative confidence. That's probably because it's an uncharted territory for them. Maybe they are in a job they don't consider to be creative, and they haven't had time to put their ideas to good use. But I'm sure they are still using them every day, unconsciously.

Sometimes, I have taken an idea and sent it out into the world, and I have got positivity in response to it. Sometimes, I don't get any positivity, but does that diminish the value in freely expressing yourself? I'd rather live on a stage with no audience than in a self-created cage, hiding my ideas away from everyone "just in case." Even if they don't serve me, they might serve someone else. You just don't know who your work is reaching.

Even if you don't want to turn your ideas into "work" or "success," you should still be proud of them and not be afraid to use them. Ideas are always there for a reason.

Chapter Four - Tapping into your Creative Power

Sometimes, you feel creative urges inside you, but you just don't know how to access them. I always find that time corrects that. Maybe the idea needs time to bed in and become fully developed in your imagination before you let it out. I have got frustrated so many times by this, and I've decided it's because I'm no longer a writer, or I'm no longer able to use my creativity, but it's something that always comes when you wait and do something else for a while.

I think our time is far too filled up nowadays. We don't have time to sit and think things over – unless we deliberately put aside time for it. Most of us are chained to our phones constantly – myself included, if I'm not careful. It's scary how checking a few things online can result in hours of wasted time if we aren't cautious. My grandad used to sit in a wicker chair at his window for hours, smoking. Ok, maybe I shouldn't be condoning the smoking part (even though I'm a former smoker and still secretly like it) but he allowed himself to just sit, for hours, doing nothing in order to process things. He might have been watching a tree swaying or the neighbourhood cat mulling about. He saw the neighbours coming and going. He didn't have internet, as most people didn't then, so the digital distraction wasn't there, but he used up a lot of his free time sitting and thinking, and that is a valuable pastime.

I think we are conditioned these days to constantly be working on something. We aren't encouraged to sit idly. Even when we're resting, we're scrolling and taking in information from other people. Even in our periods of relaxation, we are still being fed other people's views and drama. I always feel like I've wasted the most time when I end up sitting, watching dramatised clips of news stories, or reading posts on social media that make me feel like I'm inherently not "good enough."

I try to go online intentionally now. I've got back into spending time away from my phone. There have been times when I've felt ruled by it. I hate seeing people sitting over a dinner in a restaurant, not looking at each other or talking to each other and just glued to their phones. I often wonder if what they're doing is important or valuable? Or are they just so addicted to the action of scrolling that they can't stop themselves? Are they scared to face the void that comes when their hands are empty and they're looking into someone else's eyes? Equally, I always see people out for a walk in nature, texting as they walk – and yes, I don't know what they are doing – for all I know, they are texting someone about the beautiful Autumn leaves in Victoria Park, but I can't help feeling like their phone is robbing them of so much. If you keep glancing down at the screen, you miss the little things – a leaf falling, a squirrel dashing past and running up a tree, the lady that passes you and smiles at you. Those things are truly important – as is the time spent in person with your family and friends. Your phone is not your friend – as friendly as it might present itself as sometimes – through being a useful tool. It quickly crosses over from being a tool to being the thing that dictates your existence though. I used to physically put my phone away to stop myself getting sucked into it. I'd put it in inconvenient spots – like on top of the kitchen cupboards so I couldn't reach it without fetching a chair and climbing onto the counter. Sometimes, even that didn't stop me. Now I just willingly put it away. Once you develop a new habit with it, you see the benefits of it in the time you've regained and the health you feel in your head.

I recently realised that my bad moods often stemmed from too much screentime or not enough fresh air. Blocks in my creativity often came from the same two factors. It's amazing how much setting your phone aside and reconnecting with your senses and your environment clears the passageway to your ideas becoming creations.

People always say that you get your best ideas when your mind is idle, and I agree with that. You don't have to go looking for ideas; they find you when you give them the chance to come through. But you can't block their entrance with your phone or any other digital distractions. I know that so many conveniences have come along with phones and the internet, but so many real moments have been lost too. If my kids start commenting on me being on my phone, that's my signal that I need to cut way back. If the people that are in my presence feel neglected or placed second in line to an inanimate object, something has gone very wrong – and I think it easily happens to all of us. I don't think it's something to chastise yourself for – it's just something that reroutes you when you're heading in the wrong direction.

Chapter Five – Letting the Ideas in

A couple of years ago, I read a book called "The Artist's Way" which was really life changing for me because it makes you start certain practices to aid you in uncovering your creativity. You are forced to make intentional time to let ideas come in – through writing daily diary entries and taking yourself on artist dates. It makes you shift your focus and more easily locate the ideas that are sitting latent inside you.

Similarly, being in nature is healing in so many ways. I was discussing it this week with my mum. I always feel much more grounded when I'm in a forested area. I remember reading about Japanese tree bathing – the act of going to a forest filled with trees, just to meditate and receive feelings of relaxation from being in a tree-filled atmosphere. When I feel my feet on the ground and all my senses are engaged, my mind goes quieter, and I start to see everything more clearly. I once read that trees release something into the atmosphere that make us feel calm and meditative and I have definitely experienced that. Virginia Wolff had a shed where she did her writing in in her garden so she could be surrounded by natural inspiration while she wrote. There is a reason why people go on writer's retreats – it's the same idea – creating a physical space for yourself in which to create. I think that's why I find going out to parks or cafes so helpful. Changing your external environment helps you look on your projects from a different angle and you don't get side-tracked by the other tasks that are waiting to be done in your home.

Stepping outside of your own bubble always brings creative ideas with it. Sometimes, when you're stuck in the house and everything feels stagnant, your ideas get stale too. I think physically moving gets ideas flowing again. There is so much inspiration to be found in nature. The fresh air and calming scenes bring your thoughts to the forefront of your mind and you're able to more easily filter out what you do and don't want to act upon.

If nature and weather and the seasons weren't an important part of the creative process, I don't think that people would have written about them in such detail for centuries. I have a book filled with a nature-inspired story for each day of the year. Even if nature isn't the topic of a story, it features in every piece of fiction I have read. Artists are always painting nature; it is prescribed as therapy for so many different problems and we have so many connections and associations made to it in our minds. All it takes is a single scent to transport us to our childhoods, or a glimpse of a flower that featured in our early years. When I'm walking on earth and my mind is calmed by the natural peace around me, ideas come to me in a flurry, even if they've been blocked like they're stuck in a corked bottle a minute earlier. Maybe we get stuck without ideas because we don't get as much of a chance nowadays for free thinking. We are always glued to a device, absorbing someone else's experience, or thoughts and we don't make enough room for our own. The art of doing nothing is so important for creativity. It's in those moments of boredom that the greatest ideas reshuffle themselves, so they come to the top of the pile. It's unnatural the way we are always rushing around now. There's no time to stop, never mind time to reflect, and that's what we need to expose our creativity. I know a lot of people feel like their plates are overloaded and there's nothing they can do to unload them, but there is always room for stripping back. Putting your phone away is a good start. Setting aside time to read a paper book, sitting by candlelight and asking yourself how you're feeling, lying in the bath without anything to entertain you but your own thoughts – they are all good ways to reach that creative core that exists within all of us.

Sometimes your creativity feels like it has dried up and I've learnt that it is usually due to one of two reasons – you either need to make a change in your life or you're overtired. Sometimes, I find that I just need to change my environment for the day. Everything around you can get repetitive when you've had the same routines and people around you every day. It might just take a day at the beach or a short stay in a local hotel to help you get past that. Breaking out of what has become a confinement gets your ideas moving again. You are able to find the creative energy again and everything falls into place. I can't speak for anyone else, but for me, creativity equates to happiness. The more I'm creating, the happier I am. That doesn't mean you have to drive yourself, but I just find using my mind and my hands to create anything brings me such joy. That should be the reason why we do it. There might be other opportunities and benefits that come along with it, but those are extras. Creativity is a way in which we can make ourselves happy when everything else in our lives feels out of control. It's rewarding, painting a picture for yourself. Even if no one else sees it, the act of making it is cathartic. It's like free therapy (apart from the art supplies, obviously – but I always find that you need less than you think you do.) After years of painting, I still buy cheap boxes of acrylics and canvases and sketchpads from pound shops and other discount shops. Sometimes I pick up art supplies in local charity shops. If you have the means to buy the expensive stuff, I say, go for it. But don't let lack of money prevent you doing what you feel inspired to try. You don't even need paper. You can paint on rocks, on cardboard packaging you'd usually dispose of, on the walls (if you're allowed!) My kids and I get mini magnetic canvases from the pound shop. They're great because you can paint a picture, it doesn't take up a lot of space or resources and you can display them on the fridge.

If you think of each day, with completely honesty and in a non-judgemental way, what creative acts can you name that you have done? They don't have to be limited by labels of what counts as "art." What idea have you come up with and run with? Have you made a present for someone? Have you baked or cooked something for yourself or someone else? Have you dreamt about what you might do at the weekend and made plans for it? That is an act of creativity too. You're taking an idea that pops into your head and making something tangible out of it. You're using your imagination and creativity to do something that brings you joy. That's all creativity is — no matter what the world decides to label it.

Chapter Six - Reading for Creativity

I believe that reading is an important part of the creative process. Even if you're not a writer, it furnishes you with so many wonderful ideas. And it doesn't matter what you read – it could be a cookery book, a graphic novel, a magazine or the back of a cereal box. The images and words before you will trigger something inside you. Watch those ideas forming and pay close attention to them. Don't dismiss them as "not as good" as the original writer. We are all a mixed bag of ideas and experiences. No one creates in a vacuum and sometimes the quiet reading of words is what prompts something inside you.

People are always telling me they don't have time to read, or that they simply don't like reading. But is that really true? Or do they not consider themselves to be readers because they don't read full length novels? I'd be willing to bet that most people read thousands of words a day on their phones. Even if you aren't reading traditional "reading material," you're probably reading something. Reading is the absorption and processing of the ideas of others. We make so many decisions when we are reading – we reflect on who we are, we decide whether we agree with what the writer is saying, we work out how the ideas presented are relevant to our own lives. You might read something that doesn't interest you or that doesn't speak to you, but you probably still process it in some way. It will probably still make you feel a certain way.

If you do have a creative pursuit you identify with, can you work out where the passion for that project was sparked? Mine was in reading – combined with listening to music. I read books that were so clever in their construction and that made me think, "I want to try that," so I did. I didn't do it straight away, but the idea bedded in over time. I listened to emotive songs that I wanted to incorporate into my writing. I wanted to bring the feeling of music into the words in books. Whether I've pulled that off or not isn't for me to say, but that's the primary motivation behind it. Absorbing the art of others is how we access the art inside ourselves.

When I'm feeling stuck, even if I don't turn to literature, I often turn to picture books or art collections. Just studying paintings and letting yourself reflect upon them opens something inside you. I often leave whatever I was looking at half-read or half viewed and run off to start into a project of my own. I think that there are always periods of deflation as a creative being but reinflating our mind with ideas isn't as complicated as it's made out to be. Sometimes when I resign myself to the fact that I have no ideas, that's when I begin to find them again. I pick up a book, so I can fall into the passive role of reader, but it actually engages me to the point I become an active participant in art again.

Most kids can probably remember the stories that stood out most to them in their childhoods. What did you like about them? Was it an association with the book, like with the person that read it to you? Or was it because it helped your imagination to expand? I loved the Alfie and Annie Rose books as a kid. I was mesmerised by the simple concepts and the beautiful illustrations. I remember tracing the pictures with my fingertips and reading them endlessly, until I had the stories completely memorised. Even if you don't think of yourself as a book reader, is there an early book that resonated with you? What was it about the story that spoke to you? Did it tell you a deep truth about yourself? Or maybe it just made you laugh hysterically or took your mind off your present?

I find that many people write themselves off in life as "non-creators" or "non-readers" but when you delve into the depths of the person, you often find out that that isn't true. They've probably been told that by someone in their history. Or they've decided it based on a moment of failure they connect to a book or their education. What if you allowed yourself to start enjoying books today, in any form, with no agenda?

They don't have to be a particular type. You could read a funny kids' title, or a fashion magazine, or a book of maps. There are ideas to be found within the pages of all of them – but really, they're just reminders of where to look for the ideas inside yourself.

Chapter Seven – Musical Moments

Following on from this, makes me realise that music and art are one and the same thing. They are just different forms of artistic expression. When I was younger, I didn't recognise myself as creative at all. I'd obsess over one detail in a picture I'd drawn, and I'd tell myself that it had spoiled the whole piece of work. I'd pick apart any compliment I was ever given, looking for a million reasons to prove it wrong. But I always loved music and it always inspired me. People have such diverse tastes in music, but it can speak to everyone in the same way. Sometimes when I'm feeling creatively stumped, I put on one of my favourite albums and see what comes to the surface. Sometimes silence is your worst enemy when you're trying to cultivate ideas. Your environment plays an essential role in determining the kind of art you come up with – I think. Music can determine the mood of the place in which it's played. It's a very instinctual art form. I think it centres you when you're creatively lost. Before I consciously started regularly creating things, I played music. Even if it isn't done to a high level, It still feeds your creativity.

I used to get piano and guitar lessons, and I never took them very far. Eventually, I ended up stopping my lessons for both instruments, but they expanded my knowledge and helped me to reach the creativity inside me that it can otherwise be hard to access. Sometimes when you're concentrating on doing something with your hands, it transports you to a different mental space. Ideas come more easily, and it all feels much more natural. I ended up going on to learn the drums and I found out that that was my instrument. I played in bands and got so much joy out of playing them and sticking with that instrument, but it doesn't diminish the value in playing the guitar or piano for a while. They helped me to learn how to read music and about time signatures and how each instrument fits together in a song. Not everything has to have an impressive end goal. When I was a teenager, I didn't have a phone or internet and I'm grateful for that now because I had to sit with my boredom and find ways to ease it on my own. I never feel bored now because I know what to reach for, to busy my mind and my hands.

Having music on in the background can bring up ideas that were sleeping inside us. Sometimes it just takes a quick association to spark something for us. Even if we aren't actively engaged in making our own music, we can still gain so much from having a musical creative space. If you think of your ideas that you've put into practice, have you had music around you at that time? Did a song ever prompt an idea? Did you create in a certain mood because of the music that you were immersing yourself in at that time?

Musicians often become artists and writers, or vice versa. I think that's because different art forms feed each other. They aren't dissimilar to each other and opening yourself up to finding your potential in one area often leads you into another as well. No form of art or creativity is useless, or not as good as something else. Sitting quietly working on a cross stitch picture is no less valuable than composing a song from scratch. Baking a loaf of bread with its own unique crust is no less creative than adding brushstrokes to an elaborate painting. All creative acts are worthy and deserve to be celebrated. They all bring up the same feelings of satisfaction in us and we are making something unique each time we tap into our creativity. No two cakes are the same and no two ideas are completely the same either. You can use music as a vehicle through which to reach your artistic abilities and it is important not to judge those attempts and to give them the freedom to be what they want to become.

A musical creative experiment:

Pick a genre of music that you feel most drawn to today. Play it in the background while you write down ideas, or work on something physical, like housework. See how many ideas come to you and don't dismiss any of them. Catalogue them and try it with a different type of music another day to see what results you come up with. Did it help your creative thinking? Did you notice any new ideas forming in your mind? What was the mood you found yourself in and what did you feel led to do afterwards?

Chapter Eight - When we put our Art into the World, it Becomes Something Bigger than Us

Whatever you feel drawn to is probably what you're meant to be doing. If the notion is there, it's usually there for a good reason. I believe that if you create something, it deserves a place in the world. Even if one person doesn't see its value, someone else will. I just thought of a painting I got in a charity shop of Frida Kahlo. I have no idea who painted it and they have no idea that I own it now. It was priced at £2, and it was sitting propped up behind the door, unnoticed, but I immediately liked it. I probably never will find out who painted it, but it doesn't really matter. I made a place in my home for a piece of art that might have otherwise been thrown away with the other charity shop rejects. The thought of that saddens me. I think it's really unique. It's a half front profile of Frida with a vibrant yellow background and paint splatters in the background. I instantly knew who it was meant to be, even though it isn't an exact representation of her. When I took it to the till, the guy working there handled it carelessly. "Oh, that," he said, not bothering to check the price on the back, "Just give me a pound for it." He clearly didn't understand why I wanted it and he just wanted rid of it. Clearly, the saying "one person's trash is another person's treasure" came from a situation just like that one.

The painting isn't perfect; it's a little wonky in places and the black outline is a bit wobbly too, but I love the originality of it and the fact that

29

someone took the time to make it. There will always be someone that feels that way about your creations, whatever they are. Maybe you want to bake for a local gathering, or you want to make handmade gifts for friends, or you want to create a centrepiece for your table – you shouldn't let fear stop you doing it. When you put anything you want to create into the world, it becomes much bigger than you. Your self-doubt and ego and the opinions of others don't matter anymore; your creativity will always touch someone in ways you probably won't ever know about.

You just have to look at huge brands and characters created for children to see the truth in that. I recently found out while playing a quiz game with family that Enid Blyton wrote Noddy. I had no idea that was the case, and I am familiar with the rest of her work. I recently reread the Famous Five to my children, but it genuinely surprised me that she had written a children's classic I had read as a kid that I had never linked to her. It's the same with Winnie the Pooh, or The Wimpy Kid novels. I have read them to my kids a thousand times, but I couldn't for the life of me tell you who wrote them. They've become beings of their own, separate and bigger than the artists that made them. In the same way, I couldn't tell you who is responsible for the invention of Mac make-up or Nescafe coffee. Granted, some creators are naturally linked to and mentioned with their works, but quite often, the pieces of art become something with an identity of their own. If you think of the Mona Lisa, I'm sure the painting springs to mind before even Leonardo da Vinci does, no matter how famous he is. Sometimes the name of the artist is as big as the piece of work, but that's usually when there is a consistent body of work that we immediately relate to them. Who's to say whatever idea you have in your head doesn't need to become something physical in the world? You might never know the full impact your creation brings.

It's tragic to think of authors and artists that never received any recognition for their hard work in their lifetimes. My mum always talks about Emily Dickenson, whose world-famous poems weren't known by anyone in her short time on Earth. But they have been recognised for the greatness they are now. Had she stopped writing because no one took any notice of her poems at the time, the world would have been deprived of something significant. As someone who has written so many books and never amassed a huge number of reviews or sales, I just keep churning the work out anyway. Maybe only one person will notice it, but isn't it worth it, to contribute something valuable to that one person's life? It's the same with anything we think about making but we deprive ourselves of the opportunity of creating. If your idea gets stamped out in your mind before it even fully develops in your imagination, it doesn't have a hope of making it into the world.

This also ties in with the hundreds of writers I've met in my life that don't do any writing. I always meet people that tell me they have a great idea and some day they'll write it down and it will become a book. I've even had people tell me that their book will immediately be picked up and be made into a blockbuster. And maybe it will, but not if they don't start putting to paper what they envision in their mind. That part takes discipline, but it is worth it for the creative reward. There must be so many original ideas that haven't come to fruition just because the dreamer didn't run with it and make it into something the rest of the world could see.

It doesn't matter what your creation is. Maybe you feel no inclination to create for public view or for praise or recognition. Maybe you just want to have the confidence to make a craft with your kid or make a few homemade gifts, or maybe you've always wanted to try your hand at calligraphy or charcoal drawings. It could be that you want to bring all your family recipes together in one book for your own use and for your children and their children after them. Each time you create something that can be physically viewed or held, you're leaving a little piece of yourself on the Earth – something that says, "I was here," or something that stays in the heart of someone else. If you can create something that inspires someone else, that is the greatest gift of all you can give. Being bold and fearless in putting your creations into the world creates a ripple effect and other people around you begin to express themselves more freely too. That, in itself, is a good enough reason to start doing it.

Some of the most creative people in the world are the ones that quietly and diligently work away at something, putting their heart into their work and they don't think about where it will end up or what people will think of it. It all ties in with self-belief in the end. If you believe in what you're doing and it makes you feel good, that is reason alone to do it.

Chapter Nine – Creating through Adversity

People are always talking about how hard life is – and in many respects, they are right. But you can make it easier on yourself through creating. I have attended various forms of therapy over the years, and none has helped me as much as creativity has. I remember struggling immensely after a break-up and during a mental health crisis once, and no matter how many weeks passed, the pain didn't seem to ease at all. But when I took up jewellery making and started to do it every day, it dulled the pain while I did it. And even though it felt like a completely hopeless moment in my life, at the end of it, I was happy I hadn't wasted all my time wallowing in my sorrow. I had a whole collection of jewellery that I'd made, just by making a single piece every day. I could give them away as gifts and I could see my efforts in front of me. As small as it is, it showed me that something beautiful can come out of moments of strife. If you open yourself up to creativity in your loneliest and most desperate moments, you can get through anything and you can admire what you have made on the other side of the situation.

Each time I have practised creativity during a difficult time, I haven't felt motivated to do it. I haven't felt like I had the energy to put into it and I had to force myself into carrying it out. But that doesn't matter; you should just do it anyway. Once you're lost in making something, you're fully immersed in the moment, and you are no longer able to feel pain. You're in such deep concentration that your world becomes all about the object you are working on creating and everything else temporarily fades away.

Historically, so much beauty has come out of times of adversity. But I also don't believe you have to be in a bad place to create. I used to think I could only write when I was sad, but now I think I could only write a certain mood of literature when I was sad. I think the reason it seemed easier to create prolifically when I was sad or depressed was because it felt like I had more time to fill. When you're sad, time seems to pass so slowly. You aren't enjoying yourself, so you aren't speeding your way through happy moments and enjoyment, you're counting the minutes until the pain passes. And it always eventually does, but when you're stuck in the centre of it, it's impossible to be encouraged by that thought. After a certain amount of wallowing, you begin to realise it's time to fill your life with other things. You turn to art to lessen the discomfort you're feeling. I think people do that without necessarily realising they're doing it at the time.

There is a cookery book I adore called "Midnight Chicken." It is written by a lady that tragically lost her husband at a young age to cancer. She recognised the role that comfort food played in carrying her through her grief. It mightn't have completely taken it away, but the act of cooking and eating fed her soul while she struggled through mourning the loss of the closest person to her. When something difficult happens, we have to find a way to outlast it. We have to find a way to outlive our difficult circumstances, so we look for a means of doing that every day. Our creative practice could be any number of things: keeping a diary, visiting a beach, starting a collection and seeking out items for it. I don't want to solely be defined by whatever tragedy befell me, and it is satisfying being able to look back and think "that wasn't the only thing that happened at that time," or "even though I was in unbearable pain, I still produced something positive."

The pain might have been immense, but if you can look at a memory, an experience or a collection and think "I made that happen in a bad moment," it shows you your own strength and it allows something beautiful to come from your pain. Your creative attempts always make an impression on someone, even if you dismiss them as unimportant. My grandmother was great at knitting and crocheting. She quietly worked away at it, and I don't think she ever broadcasted the fact she was doing it to the people around her when she was in the process of making. But I remember her giving us knitted jumpers and crocheted blankets and coasters as gifts. They felt really special because they were different to anything else we had received, and she had put her time and love into making them. Even though she didn't enter competitions or receive public acclaim for her creations, they still made a lasting impression on me and most importantly, they encouraged me to make my own creations. She and my mum were really good at getting us involved in creating something without taking over, and I think that is a better gift than any physical present because it accompanies you throughout your life and you can always make use of it.

Sometimes, it seems like people undermine their creative ability by stating that they don't come from a creative background, or because no one showed them how to do it. Although that might put some people at an advantage in getting started on whatever projects they have in mind, it doesn't limit it to those people. There are no "special" or "chosen" creatives. We all hold that skill inside us. And even if you undervalue your own skill, it doesn't take away from the fact that it still exists.

We all have moments of being beginners at something. There was a moment when I had to begin writing. I might have had some ideas stored up in my brain, or notions of what I might like to try to do, but I still had to start from scratch. I wrote my first novel, edited it, finalised it, deleted it, rewrote it, edited it, finalised it, considered publishing it and then didn't. I wasn't completely happy with the shape of it, but it was still a valuable learning experience.

There is an artist I love called The Purple Palace. She says you should "make bad art and take up space." There is too much emphasis placed on having to come up with perfection, or it doesn't count as a real piece of art, but everyone should get to make a mess before they hone their skill. And there will even be someone that loves the mess too. There have been times that I have painted something and I have loathed the finished look of that painting with every fibre of my being. Then, I've had someone tell me that they loved it. You mightn't understand why, and you might look at it and only see the flaws, but that is only because you knew how it deviated from original idea you had in your head of how it "should" look. Someone else looking at it with fresh eyes doesn't have that preconceived notion of what it should be. It is just new and original to them. I think being an artist is about feeling the fear of judgement and putting your work out there anyway. That part is as important as the act of creating itself.

Chapter Ten – Small Acts of Creativity

What does the word "creative" conjure up for you? If you think of it, do you immediately form a picture in your mind of what a creative person does? Now, take the sledgehammer and break up that notion of creativity. I'd be prepared to assume that it is limited in some way. There is no fixed definition of creativity. You could be creative at coming up with ways to save money, creative with day trips you take with your friends or family, creative with how you organise your books, creative with the way you serve coffee, creative with the way you write a list, creative with the way you dance to your favourite music. There will always be some expressed creativity in your life that you haven't even recognised as such because you felt you weren't allowed to consider it so.

I see examples of beautiful creativity all the time, but because they aren't framed and put on display, they almost go unnoticed. My friend made us a s'mores kit a while ago and I'll never forget receiving it because it was so thoughtful and original. I had another friend that gave me a set of kitchen scales and that became a gift of creativity. Before that I hadn't owned a set and I tended to use cups to bake, but it broadened my repertoire because I was able to make different recipes for which scales were required. Sometimes you pass on something you don't use yourself and it sparks creativity in someone else and you don't even know about the effect it's had after the moment of handing it to them.

It doesn't matter about the size or status of your creative acts; what matters is the fact that it brings you or someone else joy or comfort when needed.

My kids have been delighted on a couple of occasions to find crocheted flowers on our nature walks. We have found them tied to hedges and a note attached that asks whoever found it to take it home and that it is a random act of crochet kindness. If you think about it, creativity runs alongside kindness, because you are using your time and your hands to make something meaningful.

I am a member of a Facebook group where people always share their money-saving ideas. I see something inspiring on it every day. If you share your ideas with others, you are inspiring them to try things too. I saw a post this week about a lady who had filled her own clear Christmas bobbles with strands of ribbon for each of her children (the length of their current height) and she had named and dated each one. It was a simple idea, but I'm sure it inspired someone else to create something similar or sparked another idea in someone else using the materials they had on hand. I think that being creative in whatever way we feel inclined to adds to a chain of creativity that keeps all the creative energy around us moving and expanding. There is no such thing as a selfish act of creativity, so there is no reason to prevent ourselves putting it out into the world for other people to see and enjoy. Or if we want to keep it quiet, we can do that too. There is no right or wrong in how we express our creativity and where we allow it to lead us in life.

Chapter Eleven – Creating like Kids

I love watching kids' creativity. Small kids don't have any self-consciousness about what they make. They haven't been programmed yet to constantly critique their work and to find the flaws in it. I think they are much closer to the true essence of creativity than we are as adults. I love looking at the paintings in my daughter's classroom window when I'm waiting to pick her up from school. Even though the kids have all been given the same subject or the same task, there are huge differences in style of each piece. I think all kids are natural artists. As adults, it's hard to stop ourselves editing as we go. I'm guilty of doing it at times when I'm writing. The more I just write and let it flow without putting restrictions on what I'm saying, the better I find it ends up being. You should treat art and creation like an expression of feeling and instinct, rather than a controlled experiment. The more you can let go of worrying about the end result, the better it becomes.

I used to get so frustrated when I was painting that it almost took all the enjoyment out of it. I had a rigid idea of what a painting should look like and when it deviated from that, I thought I'd done something wrong. But then I realised, the imperfections are the things that actually create your own distinctive style. It's the kind of thing others can't easily replicate because it takes your eye and your hand to produce it. Once I managed to stop obsessing about the outcome, the process was far more enjoyable, and I was actually happier with the outcome too. I no longer look at something I've made and think of all the "shoulds" of what I think it could look like. I just appreciate it for what it has become, and in a way, I detach from it when it's finished, like it has become something of its own. I've realised that I don't have to like the things I make. I'm allowed to produce things that I don't think are perfect. But even though I don't have to like them, in a way, we should love our own creations. I'm inspired by kids in that way. They are always so proud of what they've made when they're little. You never see small kids picking over the things they hate about their art. They just gush about how great it is and then they move on to something else. That's what I aim to do in my own life, and I think it's probably one of the keys to happiness too.

Now that my daughter is getting older, I can see her starting to pick apart her artwork. She was always quite confident with it – probably because she felt like it was her "thing." Now she has gained an awareness of comparison and judgement and that saddens me a lot. I want to encourage her to still create freely and not worry about the outcome. I know how hard it is to do that though. For me, it was something learned through practice – and it took a long time for it to begin to click. I still have self-doubt, but I've stopped hating every word I add to a book or every picture I add to a blog post. I just let them be what they are. I remember her bringing one of her paintings home for me in P1. I still have it on the wall. It is a lovely picture of a teddy bear, and I think it's quite advanced for her age and expected ability. But I equally love the paint splat paintings and the rushed artwork of my younger daughter. Her paintings usually look like a brief interlude in the middle of another game she was playing, that she then rushed off to complete instead – and there is so much of her personality in them.

We don't have to be named the "best" at what we do to do it anyway. And there is no "best" anyway. That is just an illusion. It's one of those bars that has been set to discourage people and to weed out the competition. If we all created in whatever way we felt naturally inspired to do, the world wouldn't be a poorer place; it would be much richer and there would always be room for everyone's art. It's like whenever I see my daughter's class's artwork in the classroom window. Each piece is different and there is room for all of them to shine in their own way. Each picture tells a story of its own about that child and each one is equally valid. It doesn't become invalid because one child was selected as top of the class and given a certificate. I think schools have become better at being balanced about things since I was there, but even if one award is given – sometimes it's deserved – or sometimes it just fits with whatever is conventionally considered to be good or whatever that teacher is looking for at a particular moment.

I remember developing a certain amount of self-consciousness about art in primary school, and I think that came from knowing who the talented people were and knowing I wasn't counted as one of them. But that doesn't have to define you. Just because one teacher failed to notice your sparkle, it doesn't mean that it isn't there – or maybe they were just looking for something else. Sometimes it isn't personal, but it can feel so. I can remember constantly using my hand as a shield between my work and the teacher's eyes as they looped the room to inspect our efforts. I really lost confidence in drawing pictures, even though it was something I'd always enjoyed doing. I couldn't draw perfect cartoons out of my head, which at that time, meant I couldn't do art on the whole. Even though there is a place for cartoon designs, that is not the only valuable form of artist expression, and I think we can see the full picture of that in adulthood. It would have made school easier, knowing it then, but we can give ourselves the encouragement now that we might have lacked at that impressionable age. It's never too late to start encouraging ourselves and being our own cheerleaders.

The more you do, creatively, the more confidence you will gain. It happens without you even realising that it is occurring. It's like the progression from learning a few notes on the piano to playing an entire piece of music. It is all learnt incrementally, and it comes together the more you do it. I think it's just about finding a passion inside you that keeps you trying and learning, and then you'll become good at the thing you love without even realising it has happened to you. You just need to be brave at first and work through the self-doubt.

As I mentioned earlier, I have loved painting since school, when I gave it up before A Level because I didn't get my predicted grade. I let that be a huge blow for years, but it didn't stop me drawing and painting in my free time. I got back into an art class when I was living in Glasgow, and I got to try new techniques and gain a little more confidence to try again. The artist that took the class had to write a report for each of us at the end of the block of classes. I remember he wrote that he could see promise in my painting. That gave me a little boost that made me decide to continue trying. It mightn't have taken me anywhere big on paper, but I now paint every week and I'm regularly filling acrylic pads and canvases. I'm doing the thing I wanted to do but that I didn't think I was good enough at to have the right to do.

One of my favourite films is "Harold and Maude." Although it seems morbid and twisted at first, the underlying message is so positive and inspiring. I love Maude's character and I remember one of her lines was "how the world still dearly loves a cage." That phrase is true in so many senses. The world likes to restrict us and entrap us in whatever small corner we are familiar with. People feel safer when they can easily define others – particularly when they struggle with their own insecurity. But we always reserve the right to knock down the bars of our worldly cage and create our own artistic space.

When I'm feeling very creatively blocked and I can't get to the bottom of what is causing it, it's always something that is easily corrected. Our adult minds like to over-complicate everything, but sometimes, it's as simple as going for a quick walk or painting a picture like a happy kid. Those simple and easy tasks help to release something in us that was starting that ugly internal loop of self-criticism again.

I think that kids have a much clearer view of what creativity should be like than we do. We are always over-analysing and justifying what we do instead of just doing it.

Just do it.

Chapter Twelve – The Danger of Devices

I have always enjoyed reading books about inspiration and getting creative. Even if you've thought of the ideas yourself, it helps to have them compiled at your fingertips whenever you're struggling to access your own ideas. I do believe that creativity comes in waves for most of us. It's just the nature of it. You need periods of activity and periods of rest and thoughtfulness. The same can be applied to anything else too. It's just the natural ebb and flow of life.

I used to get really frustrated with myself when I felt I was lacking in creative ideas. I would think it signalled the end of a road, rather than just a bend in it so you can slightly change course. The ideas never dry up. They always resurface again – usually the less you force them to. I have grown to love inactivity. I think there is far too much emphasis placed on activity in our culture in the UK. I know that people say they are embracing slower lifestyles, and maybe select groups of people are. But when I look around, most people have their heads bowed to their laptops or phones – feverishly typing away. And maybe they're working on something satisfying, but usually they have a look of intense strain on their faces. It's hard to believe that any happiness is to be found there.

Quite often, when I'm not writing a book or working on a blog post, I take a paperback or my journal to a café. There is something so grounding about flipping the paper pages of a real book or making your own pen marks on paper. It sounds like quite an obvious thing to do, but I rarely see anyone else doing the same. In fact, it has become so rare that one day, in Tim Hortons, a man approached me just to tell me how happy it made him, seeing me writing in a notebook. He said you never see it anymore. When I scanned the room, I realised that he was right. Without exception, everyone in the room was typing or texting, or just looked lost in their phone. They almost have a zombified look at times, like their faces have lost all defining individual features through mindlessly scrolling and liking everything – probably without questioning whether they do, in fact, like whatever it is.

I don't say this from a place of judgement. I've been there too, and I regularly have to make a conscious effort to claw my way out of that pit. Sometimes, it takes a while to realise that it has even happened to you again. Usually, I'll notice it by my mood. When I'm in a foul mood for no reason and I don't feel like I have the free time to spend with the people in my immediate vicinity, it's a warning sign that I need to detox from the call of my electrical devices again.

I think there is a direct link between internet usage and a loss of your own creativity. Although I might get ideas online, they are always put on hold while I disappear down the rabbit hole that is the internet. I also find that apps are set up that give the impression of feeding your creativity, when actually, in a way, they're starving you of it. Maybe they are useful in the more passive phases of your life, but sometimes they give you the impression that you have already practised creativity, when in reality, you have just absorbed someone else's. An example of this is Pinterest. It is filled with great ideas, and it can be a source of inspiration and entertainment. But I don't often use it now because it just leads you from one link to the next – part of a never-ending chain that drains all the time from your day. I don't know about everyone else, but whenever I get one of those notifications from my phone that says my screen time has gone up to an average of five hours a day, it really depresses me. It acts as a wake-up call too though. It shows me in undeniable terms that I have been wasting thirty-five hours of my week just messing about on my phone. (And that is usually exactly what it is – it isn't spent in great online productivity.) Considering the fact that there are only 168 hours in a week and a good number of those are spent sleeping, that's a worrying amount of time given over to the god you've made of your phone or tablet or computer.

Usually when I spend too much time browsing ideas online, I end up feeling creatively wanting rather than inspired into action. I think there is a definite crossover point between valuable time spent online and dead time online. I usually find that using the internet as a tool, for example, in creating a blog post or a video, in searching for new reads, in getting unique gifts for people, is better than just using it as something to fill a void and what becomes a lazy use of time. And the thing is – I don't think anyone ever sets out to waste time online, but they get swallowed into it and they don't even realise until hours have passed. I think it can be helpful for design, inspiration and creativity in small doses, but it's sometimes hard to measure out those doses for ourselves. It requires a lot of discipline. I love putting my phone out of reach at certain times or in an inconvenient spot and using that time for something else. It's amazing how much housework or other productivity that can occur in that time. What I might have called creative time with my phone positioned beside me was really 90% scrolling, 10% creating. If the distraction is removed, at first, it feels very uncomfortable and it feels like you're being faced with yourself at your rawest – but the discomfort passes, and it leads to so much satisfaction and artistic expression.

Everything in our society is so fast and instantaneous and creativity is often the complete opposite to that. The process of creation takes time and slow consideration. It has become a feeling that is unnatural to us, but that doesn't mean that it isn't good for us. Sometimes the things we immediately reach for are the most damaging things to us.

I don't make new year's resolutions, but I'm constantly renewing my resolution to keep my screen time to a minimum. Its something that constantly needs to be checked and moderated. It's such a drain on all our spiritual resources – and by that, I mean our emotional energy, our ideas and our individuality. If we give too much time to our devices, we risk becoming roboticised versions of who we're meant to be. In order to access our creative power, we need to set down the distractions first, and that is no easy task because they are everywhere nowadays.

The Ulster Folk Museum in Northern Ireland always inspires me when it comes to paring back our lives and recentring ourselves on what our purpose is. It's such a slow-paced place. I love walking around the town and the countryside there, exploring the old houses. Most of them are a couple of hundred years old and they don't have any of the home comforts we have today, but somehow, I feel like the people that lived there were richer in lots of ways. There's something really calming about walking into a cottage with no noise but the crackling of the fire and the sound and smells of cooking. The people that work there are dressed in costume and playing the roles of our ancestors. They have slower days. Even the workers seem to have time to think. There's a man that creates wicker baskets and huge wicker sculptures. He potters away at his job all day, coming up with so many unique objects that most of us in modern society would never get the time to make. There is a fire burning in the background, there is no TV or radio playing, no company from other workers – he's just alone with his willow and his thoughts.

I recently spoke to a lady that was making rag rugs. She just had some hessian bags, a single rug tool and some scraps of fabric and she was making something so useful and unique with them. When we were there, she was making a rug with a star motif on it, and she said it would be used in one of the houses when she was finished. There was so much more creative freedom then and people displayed their efforts with much more pride than they do nowadays.

Chapter Thirteen - Over-Availability of Materials

In modern society, we have access to so many materials and so many options, but sometimes it feels excessive. There are huge hobby stores with every craft under the sun. I don't often venture into one – even though, in a way, it's my idea of heaven – but it's so easy to overspend and over-collect. You can buy paint supplies, clay, card-making materials, calligraphy supplies, drawing tools, spray paints, children's crafts, sewing supplies; the list is inexhaustible. If you have an interest in every area, it makes it harder to narrow down what you truly want to focus on. It becomes easy to pick at things but never become fully immersed in one project. I've been guilty of this. I believe there is value in learning new things, even if you don't become a pro at them. I attended calligraphy classes with a friend for a number of weeks and I really enjoyed it. But have I picked up an ink pot since? No. There just aren't enough hours in the day. I toy with the idea of getting really good at knitting or crocheting, but I started to crochet a coaster about two years ago and haven't returned to it since. Trying different crafts and projects isn't a waste of time, but if you want to see anything through, I think the over-availability of materials makes this much less likely. Had you lived in a remote cottage two hundred years ago, there wouldn't have been a never-ending supply of paintable polystyrene eggs and cross-stitch kits. You might have had an embroidery hoop, a needle and thread and some material. You had to use whatever was on hand, but that didn't stop people creating. It forces you to use your creative mind to come up with the means to create, instead of lazily strolling into a craft store and filling your trolley with everything you see.

Since there has been a cost-of-living crisis, I have seen people putting so much more time and effort into coming up with creative alternatives to what they used to buy. With Christmas approaching, I have seen lots of posts of people making their own Christmas crackers with items found around the house, people have been foraging for holly and ivy and making their own Christmas wreaths. We might feel like we have lost certain luxuries we took for granted for a long time, but we are getting closer to our creative centres. We are getting into the mindset of people that made so much with so little decades or centuries ago. Sometimes, the less you have, the more you come up with, because you're forced to get creative, and that is a gift in a way. It shows you just how far your ideas can carry you and how much you can come up with, with limited resources.

One of the things I do find social media useful for is the groups you can share ideas with others on. I am a member of a group called "Scrimping on a Budget" and it is a goldmine for creative ideas and money-saving tips. People often give away materials they aren't using online too. I saw that someone had posted some holly cuttings from their garden a few days ago, offering them to anyone that wanted to make a wreath out of them. Having limited supplies brings out the kindness in people too and encourages people to share what they do have. I like to scour charity shops for gems too. You can find so much around you and so much in your home for your creative endeavours when you look at everything in a different way. There have been so many times that I have gone to a shop to buy a "needed" item and then I have found one stashed away at home, or something else that serves the same purpose.

Creativity brings so much richness into your life and it reminds you of what you already possess. I think that when we are distractable and living in the race that so many people around us are running, we feel like we are lacking so much, but what we are really lacking is time and the opportunity to mull things over and hear our own internal voices. That voice is the one that guides us to our creative inner worlds.

Chapter Fourteen - Putting Pen to Paper

When I'm feeling creatively blocked, I find brainstorming on paper so useful. When you're stuck on a certain, very particular idea, it helps to broaden your vision and look at all the off-shooting ideas that come from it. Writing without consciously thinking is often where we can find our best ideas and our truest desires. I think that's why in "The Artist's Way," so much emphasis is placed on writing daily morning pages. If you write in a stream of consciousness way, you'd be surprised what comes up and what your most dominant thoughts are. It's a practice I'm not good at keeping up with every single day of the year, but when I remember to do it, it makes a big difference.

I think that writing physical lists is really helpful too. It helps to unclog your brain and get your thoughts moving again. Sometimes I think the strain of our busy lives impairs us with regards to accessing our best ideas. You almost need to be removed from the mania of the world to get a chance to take a breath and hear your own thoughts. There are certain practices I find centre me when it comes to accessing them. Lighting a candle and sitting in a quiet room is hugely helpful, as is putting on some music that always inspires you. Lying in the bath can be a great place to find your ideas and then you can scribble them all down while they're still fresh in your mind.

You don't have to be a writer to benefit from writing words on paper. I find writing cathartic and I know it's an area in which I have a lot of interest, but even if you don't, journalling, making lists or just sketching or scribbling are good ways to access your inspiration. I think there is a good reason the medium Tyler Henry scribbles when he's visualising and looking for messages. Making use of your hands frees your mind up to absorb and process information. Whether you believe in mediumship or not, the idea remains the same – putting pen to paper is a way of reaching whatever vision you want to see. It helps you to plough through all the mess surrounding your purest ideas and to find them, like finding a pearl hidden from view behind masses of seaweed and enclosed in a clam shell. You're physically chiselling your way closer to what you're meant to create.

I have so many notes that I'd never want anyone to see – mainly because they're a disorganised, unedited mess. But I think those notes were essential in honing my skills as a writer. It's like purging all the rough outer edges of ideas so you can reach the pure, crystallised ones.

A creative exercise

Write down whatever is on your mind. Do it messily and don't allow yourself to overthink it. Let your hand wander across the page before your mind has time to catch up. Are you surprised by what you've written? Have you uncovered a truth about yourself that you didn't want to acknowledge? Have you found your number one priority in this moment? Try to do this for a few minutes each day and see what changes in your life. Don't let your conscious mind control what you want to say. If you don't have the words to write, just doodle or scribble and see what comes out.

Chapter Fifteen - Spirituality and creation

Whether you're a spiritual person or not, spirituality and creativity are inextricably linked. When I say that, I'm not talking about organised religion, or religious beliefs in any form. I'm talking about something unquantifiable that you know within yourself in your most meditative moments. You don't have to believe in a god to be creative but being connected to your highest self helps you to be creative. I know that that sounds very intangible and "hippy," but bear with me.

What I think of as a person's highest self is the version of themselves that they want to be if life didn't get in the way. Think of your deepest desires and the way that you'd want to comport yourself if there were no limits in place. Think of your truest thoughts and the moments that you have felt the closest to your own soul. There are a million ways to get that feeling. Sometimes, you need a little help to reach it. If you've been going through life in a zombified state, working yourself into the ground, neglecting your health or prioritising material things, you're probably further away from that real self. The more authentic you allow yourself to become, the more creativity will come to the surface too. Think about what motivates you to be creative. If it's competitiveness, that might drive you to work hard, but it won't bring forward your most authentic ideas. Usually, being the best version of yourself that you can be is what brings ideas to the forefront of your mind. Whenever I feel creatively stumped, it is usually because I am blocked in another way, emotionally. I think creativity and feelings are deeply connected and one is a clear indicator of what's happening with the other.

Whenever I'm feeling stuck in that way, I know it's time to change something. It can be something as simple as going to the beach and clearing your mind, or maybe you need a short holiday in a different environment to get everything moving again. When my kids grow up, I'd really like to go to a writer's retreat. I'd even enjoy renting an Airbnb in peaceful surroundings just for the purpose of writing. I know that other writers like to attend conferences and writing retreats in large groups. Truthfully, I don't know how those are run, but I prefer the idea of working peacefully in my own small space. The smaller the space the better – there are fewer distractions around.

As I covered earlier, I feel most disconnected from myself whenever I'm too connected to the internet. It's a way of numbing your feelings and finding a quick pick me up, but it's rarely deeply satisfying. I think the more you give your energy to other things, the more it drains away from you. Maybe that's why whenever people are over giving they don't feel like they have anything left of themselves. I've noticed as I've got older that I need to be selective about where I dispense my energy. I can't afford to liberally fling it around me like confetti. If I do, I just find myself with an empty container and no joy left to sprinkle on myself. Keeping some of that for yourself is what enables you to spread it further anyway. If you have energy left, you put it into thoughtful projects: a book that inspires someone, a handmade gift, a handwritten letter to someone you love.

There is a lady whose style I loved called Ilona Royce Smithkin. My mum introduced me to her through Advanced Style, which celebrates unique personal style in older women. She was more than one hundred years old when she died, and she was still so vivacious. She wore different coloured false eyelashes that she changed all the time and colourful clothes that were almost ceremonious in their presentation. She was an artist, and she was always inspired and working on something, whatever her age. I was saddened when I heard that she had passed away, but you couldn't say that she hadn't led a long and fulfilling life. My mum's favourite quote of hers was "Don't over-give, over-thank or over-apologise." At first glance, it might seem like a selfish way of living, but if you think about the words, it is really just a sensible outlook to have and probably a big part of why she lived such a long life. You're conserving the energy you need for yourself first, so you have more to give to the world. That's the greatest gift you can give the world anyway – being the most authentic version of yourself. If you do that without striving, you're sending out positivity in a way that has a huge ripple effect.

Think of all the people that seem the happiest to you and the most satisfied with their purpose in life. Where do they direct their energy? Do they overdo anything, or do they have healthy boundaries set for themselves? They are probably very selective about what they take on and about what they step back from. That isn't selfishness – it's self-preservation. There have been so many times when I have tried to please everyone around me and keep up with the requests that were being fired at me from all directions. I just ended up stressed and snappy. I've also noticed that I get ratty when I'm not creating. It's something I have to do to feel aligned with myself. When I don't feel that way, it's a big signal that something is very wrong. You might be managing to keep everyone else around you happy, but are you ever happy yourself? Trying to keep juggling so many plates always results in them coming crashing down around you in the end. It doesn't matter how skilled you are at it; even a juggler can't juggle forever.

It might seem like I'm deviating from the subject of creativity here it's all inextricably linked. Time, energy and feelings are all tied to creativity and if you don't have what you need, you can't create – at least not easily.

There are times when I know I have to be disciplined to achieve what I want. Maybe I desperately want to finish a book. Usually, I get a niggling feeling in the back of my head and I'm obsessing over plot details when I want to relax. Getting them out of my head and onto paper is the only way to still my mind. There is a quote of Sylvia Plath's about her reason for writing – "I have a voice inside me that will not be still," and I can completely relate to this. It's a feeling of disquiet that doesn't go away until you've finished a project. It's not necessarily a negative thing – it's the thing that makes you get projects completed. But everything needs to be balanced. After periods like this, it's important to take rest and to allow your thoughts to wander far and wide and away from the narrow framework of whatever story you've been creating. You need to check in with yourself and see how you're feeling in terms of your energy levels, your mood and your time. If anything feels off kilter, it's a good sign that something needs to shift.

We live in a very driven society. Little value is placed on pursuits for which we aren't paid. There have been so many times when I have felt like what I've been doing has been dismissed as unimportant because it isn't drawing a real wage. But just because the world tries to convince us of that, it doesn't make it true. Being a mum, cleaning your house, painting a picture, reading a book – they are all valuable uses of time. I think that many things that are rewarded with money aren't good uses of time – attending meetings you hate, typing emails you don't care about, running around to the point of endangering your life just to keep up with all your tasks. Why are those things celebrated when a slower life isn't?

I think we have moved away from creativity in many ways. We are led to believe that we are being creative, because we are posting on Instagram or looking at pictures or commenting on threads, but really, we are just wasting energy we could be using on making things that last, or that at least bring us joy as we are making them.

I think that being creative and making whatever comes into your head leads you to a better spiritual space too. You're following your instincts and even if you make something you don't love, you're still following a prompt inside you, and it's there for a reason. When I work through projects, I usually share them with others now, because you never know whom it might reach and what value it might bring. If it does nothing but inspire someone else to try to write a story of their own or it helps someone to understand an underlying issue of theirs that remains unresolved, it's worth it. When you create, you're being guided by your inner voice, and it all serves a purpose.

Life is so busy nowadays and we are all so distracted that we don't get a chance to stop and think about things – like our place in the world, our non-money-making ideas and our spiritual wellbeing. Slowing down and getting creative reconnects us with all those important things. If you eliminate all the noise around you and focus on one thing you're making with your hands, it's surprising how much it can bring up for you.

Last night, I worked on a painting I really don't like. In fact, I hate it so much, I'm sure it will end up in the bin. But the process of painting was still enjoyable, and it gave me the headspace I needed to calm everything down. When I'm immersed in doing something like that, the mental chatter dies down. I don't think about anything but the colour mixing and brush choices. It's the time I'm most likely to have an epiphany about something – and it's often something I've been confused about for a long time or that I've spent hours or days mentally wrestling with, to no good end. Creativity brings a level of mental clarity that ordinarily seems difficult to access – at least, that's my experience of it.

Chapter Sixteen - You don't Have to Enjoy Making Toilet Roll Tube Dogs to be Artistic

There is a common misconception that people need to be good at kids' crafting to have any sort of artistic ability. I don't know where this stemmed from, but I remember a girl in school whose mum was a teacher with a degree in art. She was considered to be naturally gifted at art too because she was "following in her mum's footsteps." Her mum was the kind of mum that loves to make junk art (I guess I have become that kind of mum too.) But I do it with my kids because I enjoy doing it; it's not out of a sense of obligation. I don't believe you should have to force yourself to be interested in something you're not. Some people grimace at the thought of PVA glue on their fingers and that's ok. Just because you don't channel your creativity into that specific task doesn't mean that you aren't creative.

Before I had kids, I genuinely believed that I was terrible at crafts. My mum used to do card making with us and she had all the tools for it. She even had a hot glue gun and an embosser, and she was really good at it. She could have sold her cards, they were so special. But I was really bad at it. Even though I appreciated having the chance to make them with my mum and sister, it just left me feeling frustrated. I didn't feel like I could do it and my cards always ended up with grubby gluey fingerprints on them, or stamps that hadn't printed properly. I had no confidence in my ability to do it and with each card I made, it worsened. It was like I was proving myself right about how bad I was at it with every greeting I added – and that negative self-talk made me hate the activity too. When

I looked at my mum's masterpieces, I felt inadequate, and I told myself I just "couldn't do crafts."

I believed that when I had kids, I wouldn't be one of those mums that crafts with their children. It felt like there was a lot of societal pressure to do it – not to mention the pressure coming from Pinterest alone. But I just didn't feel like I had the desire to do it. In my mind, it would be like mentally reliving the feelings of failure I had attached to crafting. I had unconsciously created a lot of comparison and pressure around making crafts and it made me dread it. I remember my kids' dad suggesting I make something with my daughter and I practically grimaced at the idea and told him I didn't know where to start with it.

But slowly, over the years, I've grown to enjoy what I once hated, just by doing it. Craft projects have been sent home from school to be completed as homework, and I've realised I derive as much enjoyment from it as the kids do. I think a big part of allowing yourself to create is letting go of perfectionism and the fear of failure. If you make something you don't like or that doesn't work out as planned, what's the worst thing that can happen? If you really hate it, you can scrap it and start again, or you'll know what you want to do differently next time. My kids and I have made some monstrosities, but we enjoyed the process of making them. That's the main reason to create – it's getting something out of your system and playing around with ideas.

If you don't want to make a farmyard out of items from the recycling bin, you aren't a failure as an artist. There are a million different ways to create, and one way isn't more valid than another. I've met some very creative people, as everyone probably has, and I've felt small in their presence plenty of times. When you see someone else confidently creating in front of you, it makes you feel like you can't live up to the same standards. It's easy to write creativity off as "not for me" when you see someone achieving it to a level you can't imagine yourself ever doing. But one person's talent and promise doesn't take away from our own – not unless we allow it to, at least.

Confidence doesn't come naturally to everyone, so not everyone will feel a sense of conviction in what they're doing. You just have to keep doing it anyway. That's the only difference, in my eyes, between someone that is creative and someone that isn't. They don't push through the uncomfortable feelings to start bringing their ideas to fruition. Whenever we stop setting limits on what counts as "art," we are able to unlock access to whatever it is we truly have an interest in or a passion for. If you hate making junk model animals – don't – but don't write yourself off as "not a creative person" because of it.

Chapter Seventeen – The Creative Tap Never Runs Dry

Maya Angelou said "You can't use up creativity. The more you use it, the more you have." I have grown to agree with that statement. I used to think you could run out of ideas or use them all too quickly. And whilst I believe that "burn-out" is a real thing, I don't think that running out of ideas for good is. You are always getting ideas. The only thing you need to do to is notice them passing through your mind and avoid being dismissive of the ones that aren't fully formed yet. The bitty thoughts are often the foundations of grand ideas. They just need time to grow and cerebrally develop first. Once you get into the habit of frequently practising creativity, the more you feel the need for it in your daily life. You get a thirst for creation that can't be satiated. The more books I write, the more books I want to write. If you look at most people that create something, there are very few that create one thing and then never create again. Creativity is a mindset that it's hard to switch off once you've turned it on.

It's ok to start small with your ideas and to test things out. You don't have to make a masterpiece on day one – or ever - to have permission to create. It annoys me when people take it upon themselves to create closed circles of artists where you need an art degree and a portfolio to prove your right to entry. I don't know how these groups are established, but I think they're more damaging to creativity than they are inspiring. It makes it feel like it's some sort of club you can't gain access to unless you are "good enough." But what makes someone "good enough?" And I have met so many inspiring and creative people whose ideas aren't backed up by rave reviews. That doesn't diminish what they're doing. It's taken me a long time to learn what creativity is. For a long time, it felt like something that couldn't be defined, but it's just a practice – a decision to keeping making things.

Once you open the door to your own creativity, it's hard to fully close it again. There might be times where you're in stasis and you aren't making anything, but the desire to create always resurfaces. One creative act feeds another. Think of a time when someone you know did something to inspire you. Did you go on to make something of your own? For example, if someone gave me something homemade, it would inspire me to return the favour. One person makes something, and it brings that idea to the forefront of your own mind. Sometimes creativity is even just giving someone else the means through which to be creative. I have a good friend in Glasgow and when I used to live there, she'd bring me bags of apples from her parents' apple tree each year. I was so grateful for the gift because it inspired me to make apple crumble and to exercise my own creativity. Sometimes the best thing you can do for someone is to give them the keys to unlock their own creativity. When I lived in Scotland, I had a lot of hard times, but creativity always came along to take me by the hand when I was feeling a bit lost. At different times, I found art classes, cooking, baking, jewellery making, playing drums in a band and many friends inspired me along the way with their personal creativity. No matter what you might lose in life, no one can take your ideas away from you. If you keep focussed on them, you can survive so much because they give you the boost of hope you need to keep moving forwards.

I always enjoyed doing certain creative activities – I loved playing drums in a band, I loved playing around with music at home, I enjoyed keeping journals and writing poetry, but it wasn't until I started practising creativity every day that I felt the need to do it more and more. When you begin with one creative goal you want to attain and you work towards that, it becomes like a drug. I suppose it's the same as going to the gym is for certain people. (that will never be me!) It just gives you such a sense of accomplishment when you see something through, or when you spend your evening putting paint on paper without pausing to question how it's going. It's like developing any other habit – but this one is much healthier than a lot of others. One creation is the beginning of a long chain of creations. It becomes such an integral part of your life that you no longer know how to be happy without it. You crave that feeling of satisfaction that comes with a completed project, so you start more, and more and even when you try to stop, you find yourself daydreaming about the next one.

It's better to start something you might find imperfect and get it finished than it is to keep perfect-looking dreams in your head forever. If they never materialise into anything, they just disappear, and they'll never be seen by anyone. That's much sadder than the notion of producing something that falls short of your idealised version of what it could have been. You'll probably end up appreciating it for what it is anyway. And just think about other people's ideas of perfection. For example, if someone gave you homemade sweets would you obsess about the fact that they were asymmetrical or unprofessional looking? No, you'd just be delighted to have a handmade gift and something different that no one else has.

What you create doesn't always have to be in the same vein either. For years, I struggled with that idea. When I started to identify as a writer, I felt like any other creativity I engaged in was detracting from my writing. I wanted to hone the craft and learn everything I could, in order to improve, but that doesn't mean you should sicken yourself with your primary focus. I used to think that if I baked or coloured in one of those adult colouring books, or read a book, that I was neglecting my craft. But one creative project nourishes another, even if they are unrelated. Sometimes I find that baking cookies gives me a much-needed break from writing, and having cookies to go along with the coffee that accompanies my writing is an added bonus.

If you exhaust yourself, you can't easily create anyway. When I do too much and burn myself out, I feel like I'm left with an empty mind and unmanageable emotions. Making some time just for yourself, to make yourself feel better is a good use of time. Not all time needs to be spent on something that earns you money and wins praise from someone else. It's important to spend time moving along creatively, feeding your soul and keeping yourself engaged in satisfying pastimes.

Creative Practice

Start one little project today, however small and see where it leads you to. Can you identify the chain of creativity and how one activity inspires the next? Keep a diary about it for a month or two and watch your creative growth. It doesn't have to be anything that would win you an award – it could be something as simple as sketching each day, baking different kinds of breads or making cards for friends. Or maybe you want to cut out ideas from a magazine and make a dream board, or learn how to crochet, or come up with some new recipe ideas for dinners. There is a lady whose YouTube channel I love (Coffee with Kate) and she is always recommending books about cooking and frugality. I ordered the Tightwad Gazette after hearing her singing its praises. It's a bit outdated in certain ways, but it is like a catalogue of creative solutions for people with few financial resources. It shows how to do things like throwing a child's birthday party on a budget. Decorations are made using materials that are already in the home. The book comprises hundreds of letters from people that wrote into the original newsletter sharing money saving ideas. After reading many of them, you're reminded of just how creative everyone in the world is, without even realising they are. There are so many inventive solutions that people have come up with to save money. Maybe that's the incentive they needed to come up with ideas, but it shows that people really do have the ability to make a lot out of very little and to come up with solutions other than running to the shop for what they need. I found it to be a good reminder of how much ingenuity there is around us. It's easy in our society to forget this – but when you remove the conveniences and the unnecessary trips to the shops, you remember just how resourceful and creative we can all be. Some of the ideas felt like a frugal step too far for me – like one suggestion to use binbags folded and looped together to make a skipping rope. But it's still good to know that there are creative solutions right in front of us and that we are fully capable of finding them. - even if you just begin with things around your own home and think about alternative fixes for things that you ordinarily would go straight to the shop for. The more you repeat these little habits, the more they pop up in every aspect of your life. Creativity is really just one long procession that never ends and each contribution a person adds to it keeps it travelling along. In beginning to be creative, you're adding to something we can all collectively benefit from. One creation leads to another until there is a beautiful world of creation all around us.

I honestly believe that every creation that people put out there has its value. Even if you aren't happy with it, it has a purpose to serve. It will speak to somebody, and it will inspire something else you will probably never know about. Many of the people that wrote letters to that newsletter probably never dreamt that their ideas would be put into print. They probably never could have imagined that they would be one of the ones selected to be printed in the book that was then compiled. Many of them were "just" housewives, living in rural America, and here their ideas are, being read by people decades later, thousands of miles away. (Even if I'm the only one still reading them!) The point is, if you have an idea, you should never squash it. It's a being of its own and no one has the right to do that, and you never know who might need to hear it.

People talk about bad ideas all the time. We are taught in school that certain ideas are wonderful, and others are poor offerings. Brainstorming as a class often shows us which is which. But who gave permission to teachers to label ideas "bad?" Maybe it isn't what they're looking to hear at that particular moment, or it isn't something that resonates with them, but that doesn't mean that they are inherently bad or useless.

So, grab whatever idea comes to you today, however small and act on it. See how you feel by the end of it. Is it an addictive feeling? Even if you aren't happy with how it turns out, did you enjoy the process of doing it?

Chapter Eighteen – Noticing the Creativity Around You

Taking the time to notice the creativity that surrounds us requires us to look outwardly and take in our surroundings. If you make a point of doing this sometimes, not only does it ground you in the present moment – it also makes you realise just how much creativity is out there. It's easy to think that only a select number of individuals have that skill set, but even walking down the street will reveal so many small acts of creativity to you. Maybe you'll notice your neighbour's window boxes, or the sign someone has designed for a restaurant, the advertising campaigns put together for the local café's seasonal drinks, the window displays set up in shop windows. It is everywhere. As I write this, I am sitting in a coffee shop. There are Christmas displays all around me that someone has taken the time to put together. Someone decided on the style of decorations they would use. The seating layout was thought out by someone. The old library feel of the place was dreamt up by someone. The coffee concoctions were imagined before they were put on posters. It is all a huge act of creativity, brought together by many different people's ideas.

Once you get into that way of thinking, you start to realise that anything can be looked at creatively. You start to describe your surroundings to yourself like a story. You find inspiration in that. You notice the artistry in how the light cuts through the windows and falls upon your table. You see the people around you and their individual features. You come up with stories about how you think their lives might look. You don't have to take your creative thinking in this direction, but the point is, that starting to think in that way leads you to another idea, and another, until you come up with new ideas of your own.

It becomes easy at times to get lost in the seeming drudgery of life, but if you look at the little details, every day is different and it brings surprises with it. The more you believe you can find them, the more you do. It's the same with coming up with ideas. Dreaming up ideas is something that gets better with practice. If you make a point of exercising that part of your mind every day, you will find yourself doing it unconsciously.

There was a definite point at which I recognised I had ideas about things I wanted to do, but I hadn't executed them. (Like whenever I started to write, but I hadn't yet written a book.) I made the decision to stop being lazy about carrying them out and to start doing them, whatever doubts crept into my head (and there were many, and still are.)

Self-doubt shouldn't stop you being creative. It's easy to think that you aren't naturally creative If you struggle with self-doubt, but once you recognise it as a natural part of the process, you don't fear it anymore. You still hear it, but you don't give it any credence.

I have always had a noisily negative inner voice. It could have prevented me doing everything I have tried to do. After a certain point, I realised that I didn't know how to silence it, and I realised that it would probably always be there, but I would just have to create anyway. I decided to power through the critiques. When I started to regularly paint again, I had so many negative thoughts about it. I still do. I threw a painting in the bin the other day because of them. But I still keep doing it. Sometimes I'll even find that I hate something I've painted on the day I've completed it, or after one coat, but it becomes something else after the second coat, or maybe it doesn't and I still hate it. Then, I put it away for a month. When I stumble upon it again, I realise that I quite like it after all. It's hard to see the beauty in something as you're making it. It's too easy to focus on the details that you don't like or that haven't worked out for you as planned. When you put it away for a while, you forget your expectations of it, and you move on to working on something else. When you next take a look at it, it's easier to look at it with objectivity. You can see what other people see in it – when your judgement and ideas about what it should have been have receded into the background. It's like looking at someone else's creation for the first time, and then you can find the inherent beauty in it.

I remember once in school, my friends and my sister and I decided that we would set up a stall at the school craft fair. We wanted to raise money for a cancer charity. We were so excited about our stall and we spent weeks preparing. My sister and I played jazz in our kitchen while we baked tens of tiny iced biscuits, wrapping them in coloured cellophane and tying them with ribbon. My friend made origami birds and she hung them on a jewellery tree to display them. We made some other crafts which I can no longer recall. On the big day of the sale, we carted all our stuff to school in our parents' cars, excited by the prospect of raising tonnes of money for charity, but our dream wasn't to be. Even with our central location (slap bang in the middle of the assembly hall,) our stall was ignored. We were competing against adults with established businesses, selling products that far surpassed ours in appeal. I remember another stall with kids from our school at it, but it was at a different level to ours entirely. The girls running it were originally from Hong Kong and they just had that inbuilt talent for making cute, intricate jewellery and phone charms. Their products were selling out in the first hour. People kept giving our stall a sideways glance on the way to the other stalls, but no one seemed to stop at it. Eventually, a couple of friends of my origami making friend stopped by and picked up a couple of her paper cranes. She was delighted. We made a few sales then and I thought things were really picking up, but it was the last hour of the fair and we ran out of time. It turned out that my sister and I didn't sell a single bag of the cookies we'd made. I could have cried after all the effort and love we'd put into baking them. But I guess they weren't special enough – I thought. We'd gone unnoticed. After hours of work and weeks of preparation, we made a grand total of £50. Considering that there were five of us running the stall, that figure was peanuts. We still donated it to our charity of choice, but I vowed never to try to raise money for charity by selling goods again. (Or should they be called bads?) My self-esteem took a hit after that. It was already low enough it was practically scraping the ground, but it was even worse then. I felt like everything I made was worthless and no one thought it was worth paying attention to. Gladly, it had been a team effort and a team failure, or I might have had an identity crisis over the whole thing. But that started the pattern I developed of writing my efforts off as terrible and assuming anything I made was unwanted. Those little life lessons can be incredibly damaging if you let them get in – especially when you're young and impressionable. But you can't let that inner voice take hold or it will stop you making things that were meant to be made. Call those experiences a failure if you want to, but don't let them stop you.

If you let the voice stop you creating, you're robbing yourself of so much. I used to do that, but I always ended up feeling like there was an under-utilised creative force inside me. And that's a frustrating feeling. It's better to try something and to fail by your own standards than to give up expressing yourself. I've come to that conclusion about relationships now too. It's better to allow yourself to fail at something and accept the defeat that comes along with that than to keep quiet and pretend that nothing is happening and that everything will sort itself out. You can't gain anything by sitting in inertia, in life or in art.

Chapter Nineteen – Recognising your Talents

The more people I meet, the more I notice how much they undermine their own efforts. I have had so many people approach me and tell me that they aren't creative types. To me, that's like saying that they aren't the breathing type. You can't live without creating something. If you aren't creating painted mugs, you're creating a family home, an ambiance in your work, rituals you follow each day, personal relationships, playlists, hobbies and interests. Everything is creation and no one has the right to say that what you're doing doesn't fall into the bracket of creativity. It makes me sad when people downplay whatever they have done, even though I am incredibly guilty of doing this myself. I've complimented people on things that they've made, and they have just brushed it off as nothing. For example, a friend of my daughter's grandmother recently knitted her some mittens on a string she could put through the sleeves of her coat. I remarked on how lovely they were, and the comment didn't even seem to register with her. She obviously just thought there was nothing special about what she'd done. But I could see that it was. Not only had she made something from nothing but wool – she had made a useful item of clothing to keep her grand daughter warm in the Winter and to me, that's the essence of creativity – you're making something with love and putting it out there for someone else's benefit. She just seemed to think it was perfectly ordinary – like how I feel about whenever I've cleaned the bathroom. It's funny how little people recognise their skills.

I think that if people did take the time to recognise the value of their efforts, they could do so much more. I mentioned an artist earlier that I follow and whose work I love. She is constantly putting herself out there, making more art than there are hours in the day. I remember asking her once how she dealt with self-doubt when she was creating. At the time, her response annoyed me. She said that she didn't have any and she genuinely believed that everything she made was great. I thought that was conceited of her at the time and I envied her self-confidence, but everything she makes turns to gold. People just scoop up her art the second she puts it out, and I think her success starts with her own attitude towards her work. If we all had that level of self-belief, imagine how different everything would be.

People are brave when they put their work out there, not worrying about the reception. I remember going to a market once where a man was selling his poetry anthologies at his own stall. He had carried the boxes of self-published paperbacks down there by himself. It didn't look like he had made many sales. He was being passed over for the food items on offer and the stalls selling hair accessories and custom-made chopping boards. But he stood on, facing his self-doubt. I spoke to him for a moment about his book and he undersold himself. Now, looking back on it, I think that that was the only thing holding him back from making sales. He was bravely and boldly standing there with his work, offering it to the public, but he didn't believe in what he was doing. I told him I wrote too, and he almost seemed to cower in the presence of a fellow writer – which is exactly the attitude I take when I encounter one too. We tend to assume that someone else knows more than us or that we are unqualified to stand there, proudly selling our work. But we all have the same right to be there and the same right to contribute to the world of art.

Unless you're one of those naturally confident types, it's hard to have any pride in what you're putting out there. I think it's something you cultivate with practice, and just by faking the feeling until you find yourself with it. If you don't want to sell your ideas, no one else will want to buy them. You have to get behind what you're doing and believe that it is needed by the world. That doesn't mean you have to be boastful about what you're doing, but it's important to not put it down.

For those of us to whom self-confidence doesn't come naturally, that can mean just saying "thank you" to a compliment instead of immediately belittling our creations. Your efforts aren't useless, and someone does see them and appreciate them. The more people believe in the compliments they receive, the more creative abundance is likely to abound from that. If you don't feel proud of what you do, pretend to yourself that you are. Nothing bad can come from lying to yourself that things are better than you find them. (This has a general application too; it isn't just specific to creativity.)

Chapter Twenty - Creativity isn't a Competition

Sometimes it's easy to feel useless in the presence of "creative people." I say that in inverted commas because I think we are all creative people. But those who specialise in it and do it with confidence, often as a career, can make the rest of us feel lacking in talent by comparison. I don't know when creativity became so competitive, but I think the invention of the internet has made this worse in a million ways. It has made it easier for the average person to gain access to the creative world, but at the same time, we are constantly reminded of all the competition out there – and that is how it is presented. Life is a battle to see who can produce the most impressive content now. You didn't used to get judged by your online portfolio, available to the eyes of all humanity twenty-four hours a day. The fact we can access so much inspiration with a quick dance of the fingertips might be a positive thing in many respects, but it also means we are constantly measuring ourselves against content creators. It doesn't just throw our own creativity into question; it throws the value of our lives into question, and that is really damaging to our mental health – and in turn, to our creativity.

I don't think that creativity should be made into a competition. This starts in school with pupils battling for the top grades and the remainder picking up the leftovers, but it's a flawed way to approach art. I don't think you can rank creativity, placing one act of it in the top spot and the rest in the remaining available spots. It all comes down to personal taste. Maybe you like classical art or maybe you like contemporary art, you might like realistic portraits or surrealistic images, you might prefer pottery to tapestry, or texts to handwritten messages. It all comes down to whoever is looking at it and whoever has been put in charge of grading something. Do you value technical skill over free expression? If you answer this question honestly, you'll find your own style, but it also shows that neither one is the right answer – there is no such thing as wrong art. If you're enjoying yourself, that is an act of creation in itself – you're creating joy. Some of the least conventional creatives I have encountered are the ones that inspire me the most. I always come back to my mum's friend as an example of this. We've known her our whole lives and she used to visit periodically from England before she moved back to Northern Ireland. She doesn't have a degree in art, or a job in the arts but everything she does is creative and inspiring. She creates little scenes in her home, she comes up with interesting menus, she takes us on meandering walks where we uncover little known treasures. When you come away from being in her presence, you feel like you've been creatively fed, and it allows you to tap into your own creativity. People that live like that are a gift to the world because they don't just keep their creativity to themselves; they share it around and inspire others to use theirs too.

The creativity you absorb doesn't have to be related to the kind you want to practise either. You can be a writer and spend your time walking in nature, foraging for berries and it will still feed your primary creative practice. You don't even need to have a specific practice to be creative. You can just lead a creative lifestyle. My blog "The Funky Thrifter" (thefunkythrifter.com) aims to show how to do this. You just embrace whatever creative opportunities come your way, in whatever form that might be. I find that budgeting helps me with this, because I am always scouring places for free activities to do with my kids and creative solutions to enable us to lead a rich life within our means. I think you should share your creativity, not to brag or to make others question their own creativity, but to share ideas and help to keep the creativity going for everyone around you.

People that treat it as something competitive, in my opinion, do so from a place of deep insecurity. People that are always trying to prove themselves in everything they do are trying to fix something inside themselves that is fractured. That is never the solution. No matter how much success or recognition you might gain, it isn't a substitute for quiet contentment. Competition is rife in every area, but I think it should be recognised for what it is and not be congratulated and built up as a reason to practise creativity.

Can you think of a very competitive person that is ever happy? Does one success ever satisfy their need for success? Is the feeling of success ever long-lasting? Or does it just create a pattern in which the person is driven to keep succeeding and proving their efforts are better than everyone else's? I think it's also important to ask, has someone acting out of competitiveness ever inspired you to do well yourself? In my personal experience, such types just inspire feelings of dislike. It's a selfish mode of existence and one that doesn't demonstrate the true meaning of creativity

Chapter Twenty-One – Creative Context

Speaking of the true meaning of creativity, what do you think it is? That looks like an unanswerable question, but what do you think is the point in it? Why have people kept creating throughout the ages? Why do people return to creativity when they are lost or unwell? I think it's our quickest way to reconnect with our soul. It's easy to get distracted from our purpose on Earth in the midst of all the chaos around us but getting quiet and creative helps to refocus you on what's important. It eliminates all the noise around us, and we are solely focused on whatever we are making.

Even if you think about something that mightn't be traditionally considered creative, like canning, you can see the truth in that. Canning has become really popular in America again. There are lots of homesteaders that are returning to growing their own produce, making their own sauces and preserves and canning them. If you think about what the process involves, it is incredibly time consuming, but it is all-absorbing and positive. You have to grow, harvest, cook or pickle your vegetables and then can them. You even have to sterilise your equipment, but it must be so rewarding to see your efforts in front of you when you're finished.

I think the reason that so many more people are depressed nowadays is that they have nothing to show for their time. In the past, we usually did things with our time and had something to show for it. Since people have become glued to the internet, that often isn't the case anymore. I want to be able to see the fruits of the day by the time bedtime arrives. I want to be able to see the physical things I have produced with my time and to feel like I can see that my time wasn't wasted. That's not to say that not producing something is worthless – it's so important for our wellbeing to have empty moments that we don't cram full of achievements. But in those moments, I'd rather spend an hour lying in the bath, staring at the ceiling and allowing ideas to flow than disappearing into an internet tunnel.

You don't have to have picture-worthy products to show off. I don't believe that's why we create at all. People have a tendency nowadays to do things purely for the validation they'll receive afterwards. Maybe that's because they are lacking faith in themselves and their projects but think of all the things that have been made throughout the years, not publicly acknowledged, and still valuable all the same.

I was thinking about this the other day as I was driving past some Victorian buildings in Belfast. The amount of work and detail that went into them is impressive. They didn't just build a structure – it was a work of art. You can still see the bricks with unique designs on them, recognisable features from that time period and inside, they often have distinctive ceilings and mouldings. Those houses have survived the test of time and they are still lived in and used daily. They have kept many of their original features and there were people that once made these with their hands. Those people are long gone, but their efforts are still standing. They created a recognisable style that really distinguishes Belfast from other cities. I'm sure that the same can be said of most places you visit. Nobody puts the architects or the builders on a podium, giving them medals and praise, but that doesn't invalidate their work. You can see the value of it every time you pass it and choose to take notice of it.

It's the same with anything you take under your notice. I don't know who sticks up the billboard ads, but they are often uplifting and inspiring. They give me ideas for day trips with the girls or for offers on food and drinks. They offer so much to people that pass them, but no one knows exactly whose head dreamt them up.

Creativity is something that is done for the collective good. Even whenever the individual that starts with an idea begins their project, they won't see the full scale of its importance. But someone, somewhere will be touched by it – even if it's insofar as inspiring them to make something of their own that the world needs. Competitiveness will always be there, because there will always be people that are driven and wired to compete, but we don't have to subscribe to that. We can just put our own creative attempts out there and compete with no one, including ourselves.

That's another way in which creativity can become infected by competitiveness: through competing with ourselves. Sometimes, it's easy to fall into the trap of putting one thing we have made on a pedestal and pushing ourselves to create something on that level again. For example, there might be one thing that we have made that we are particularly proud of, and we have tried to recreate it many times, but have never succeeded in our attempts to do so. Just because something is different, it doesn't mean it's bad. In the same way that difference in celebrated more and more in our society, we are allowed to produce different things. It stops everything becoming stagnant and dull. Imagine if everything you created was of equal merit and similar in style; there would be no room for growth there. Maybe you made one thing that you consider to be "perfect." That doesn't mean that everything else falls short. Your idea of perfection in your work mightn't match someone else's anyway. I have created work that I genuinely hated and when I have shown it to someone they have gushed about how much they liked it. It's often completely perplexing, but it just shows how one person's idea of perfection doesn't mirror another's.

Sometimes, getting praise too early can be damaging. We might make one early masterpiece, according to a particular teacher, or parent, or to ourselves, and we spend years trying to live up to that same impossibly high standard. Had it never occurred, we wouldn't have a point of comparison drawn up. Sometimes, I feel this way about my first book. It wasn't to everyone's taste, but out of all my books, it drew the most interest. Sometimes, I tell myself that I have lost the writing knack I once had, but that isn't the full picture. I think the reason my first book sold the best and got the best reviews was because people were curious about it. Anyone that knew me was most likely to purchase that book because at the time, they didn't even know that I wrote. Now it's old news, so unless someone is a devoted reader or a book worm, they don't tend to buy or read the others. They've satisfied their curiosity regarding my writing. But that doesn't mean that my other books are intrinsically "bad" by comparison. The first one just had a springboard to jump off, while the others are jumping off flat ground.

Chapter Twenty-Two –
Figuring Out Where to Start

If you're feeling lost with regards to creativity, it's possible it has just been under-utilised. Sometimes, we leave it behind in childhood, thinking it's something we have outgrown as adults. But creativity is something that can never be outgrown. We might think it's a waste of time in our productive adult lives, but it is never a wasteful use of time. Think about the things you fill your time with. If your free time isn't spent on creativity, what is it spent on? And does this thing bring you fulfilment? But don't chastise yourself for it either. You don't have to go from practising no creativity to being creatively productive in every minute of your spare time, and you don't have to spend all hours of the day creating to be a creative person.

Can you reflect on your childhood and the things you loved to do the most? You can probably find something creative there. Maybe you loved to draw or paint, or cook, or garden, or play make believe with your friends. Granted, the last option mightn't be feasible nowadays (unless you take up acting at least!) but it can lead you in the direction of the kind of creativity you enjoy. Maybe you want to write stories, or work on plays, maybe you want to design sets or props, maybe you want to journal about your dreams, or play games with your kids. There is a talent lying in that area that shouldn't be forgotten about. As kids, I think we are much closer to our true purpose; we just have a stronger sense of what we love. That can get clouded as we are growing up, but it's easy to uncover it again. You just have to realise that it's still lying dormant inside you. We never outgrow our creative abilities. Just because I don't feel the desire to play with Barbie dolls anymore doesn't mean I don't want to come up with any storylines. You're using your imagination all the time anyway – whether you realise it or not. Think of reading, for example. When you are reading a novel, there is only so much that is written on the page. You come up with your own visuals inside your head, to match the story. You come up with images that might differ from the author's original idea. Imagination is something that we use every day without even realising we are using it. Think of all the times you have been lost in a daydream or you fantasised about your life being different. You were unconsciously creating with your mind in those moments in the same way you did as a kid. Kids just have more confidence about tapping into it because it is actively encouraged through play, and they have more time in which to do it.

Play is another thing that is associated with childhood, but it isn't limited to it. The word "play" has so many possible meanings. It doesn't have to only apply to dolls and toy cars. It can mean playing a board game, playing around in your garden, rearranging your house like it's a giant doll's house, playing with recipes, playing with paint, or just being silly. If you want to find the creativity inside you, it's important to challenge certain notions that have been presented to us as fixed concepts. I remember feeling like I had to make myself stop playing when I started secondary school. It was considered childish and no longer age appropriate. Was there a point at which you stopped using your creativity? Or have you always used it but had doubts about what you're doing? You should allow yourself to play around with things. Start small, with something that is quick to do and that yields results. For example, you could go into the pound shop with five pounds and see what craft materials you can buy. They have a great supply of arts and crafts supplies, and if you're limited budget wise, you're more likely to buy something that takes less time to complete. You're less likely to abandon a project if it is shorter in duration, and the more you practise, the more confidence you will gain in your ability to see projects through to the end.

Allow yourself to do something for the sheer fun of it and without worrying about what it will look like when you're finished. Maybe you want to try working with clay, but you're worried about the finished product. Just allow yourself to play with clay like a child would with play doh. If something comes from it that you want to keep, that's an additional benefit – but that is not the reason for doing it. The process of playing with clay should be the part that satisfies you. Once you finish a project, it almost ceases to be yours. You're no longer working on it, and the more I have written, the more I have realised that it is the actual writing that brings the most pleasure. Yes, it is satisfying to finish a book and to see your work completed, but you're no longer working on it once it reaches that stage. I usually find that I plunge head-first into another project at this point because my life feels emptier without it. You get so used to working on something that you need something else to work on next. The completion of your project isn't what brings you the most joy – it's the process of making the next thing.

My kids rarely look at their artwork after it is finished. They might feel possessive of it and protective of it (ie, they don't want me to put it into the bin.) But I never see them holding their work, completely attached to it when it's finished. The only thing I've seen them do this with is whenever they have made a functional craft – for example, a car out of a cardboard box, or something that has a function beyond being made. Kids might be proud of their work, but they move on to the next thing quickly too. I think that's why as soon as my kids have finished making something, they have the attitude of "right – what are we going to do next?" I think I am the same way with art. There are times when you do need to rest, but once I have finished one project, I don't feel satisfied until I have started something else.

If we think about what we enjoyed doing as kids and dip into that again, we will find that playful joy we had as kids again too. That's the thing that is most needed to be creative. If you don't approach it with that energy, you won't enjoy a minute of it, and that's what you are supposed to do – enjoy every minute of it.

Chapter Twenty-Three - Stop Striving

It's hard when you've been conditioned to do everything to the best of your ability. What does that phrase even mean? "To the best of your ability?" It varies depending on multiple factors – whether you're sick, whether you're sad, stressed or tired. I have been guilty of driving myself at times, and usually, when I do, it's because I feel like I'm not "enough." When you realise that you are enough on your own, without any of the added achievements, you'll stop striving and just do things for the pure joy of doing them. Not everything is meant to be fun – but creativity is meant to be fun. Even when I'm writing about dark subject matter, I'm still enjoying the process. I mightn't find the story uplifting on the whole, but I love every facet of writing. If you have that passion in your work, you can't go too far wrong.

Our society encourages stress, sickness and exhaustion in many ways. Everything is about work. As soon as we are able to hold a pencil in our hands and to form letters, we are expected to learn and work all the time. We are expected to do our best and to perform well in school exams, but what if that is all just a distraction from the truly important things? People have to be kept on the big hamster wheel of the work world. If they're making money and have their heads to their keyboards, they don't have time to question what they're doing. You have a right to be happy. If not in the workplace, you at least have the right to be happy in your home and in your free time. I know it might differ from country to country, but overall, people are trained to work hard and make money. That is what we are taught is the key to happiness: having the money to buy the lifestyle we want. But most people with luxurious lifestyles don't have the time to enjoy them because they're too busy working to pay for them. However, if you can gain access to your creative side, you'll always have the means to feel happy. Even when I have been going through absolute misery, creating things has still brought me relief and little bits of contentment in the moments when I've used it. It's something that once you start to practice, it's hard to stop and it brings so much happiness that money can't buy. (Well apart from the money used to fund whatever supplies you need for your hobby.)

I have noticed my own tendency to strive through creating art and writing. I think it's something a lot of us get in the habit of doing in school and it's hard to switch it off. Since writing and painting are my main focuses, (outside of raising my children, of course,) I found myself striving in those areas too, even though they started out as a fun diversion. I started both activities to calm my mind and to help me to relax and process my thoughts. I wanted to share my experiences with people too – so I could encourage others and to share my artwork to uplift other people. But it's easy to get sucked into the success spiral. You start to measure your efforts by how much "success" they attract. We see filtered versions of other people's lives and come up with false narratives that make us put even more pressure on ourselves. Social media is dangerous in this respect. You are constantly forced to compare how you're performing in life with the people around you. But it is never the full story. There have been times when I have seen photos that led me to believe that someone was blissfully happy and then a week later, I hear some tragic news of theirs that no one ever would have expected from their online presence. I think this online presence is just a creation in itself. It's like a cartoon character, or another fictional character you'd find on TV. You don't have the insider knowledge of what is really going on and what difficulties people might be experiencing – you just see the smile on their face and the congratulatory bottle of prosecco they are popping open to celebrate their success. I'm not saying that we shouldn't be happy for other people's success; but we shouldn't be fixated on it. We shouldn't let it to take away from our own creativity and our own contentment.

I used to get swept up into the hysteria surrounding the release of a new album of photos from a Facebook friend. The photos would show the perfect moments, as photos usually aim to do, and I would deduce from that that I was a complete failure, and my own existence was worthless. It's quite a jump to make if you think about it. Why are we naturally inclined to judge ourselves when faced with another's success? I think the photos act as a reminder of the things we want to achieve in our own lives but that we haven't. It prods at your conscience and starts you thinking of how imperfect your own family pictures might look. Little do you know, at the same moment, someone might be looking at one of yours, wishing their lives looked more like that. Here's an example of that: when I was married, there were a few photos of me online with a baby and my husband. Although whenever I look at the photos, I see a ghost of my former self and I can read the desperation in my face, someone that didn't know the full picture might have thought I had attained the dream of my ideal family. There were moments where I wanted to appear as such, as validation to myself that I wasn't living a complete nightmare, but the reality was at odds with that 95% of the time. I clutched onto the small moments that almost looked like the picture-perfect family life, but what was going on behind the photo was horrific. A photo only ever tells a small fraction of a story, so we shouldn't base our self-worth on that at all.

Whenever I see a "perfect" photo that feels like a stab to the heart, I try to recognise it for what it is: my own insecurity and a picture that doesn't give the full story. No one's life is ever perfect in every respect: you might have the perfect relationship but have money or job stress. You might have the perfect apartment, but you have ill health, physically or mentally, or you might have a family member that is causing problems for you. No matter how wonderful everything looks, life is more complex than that, so there has to be more going on there. I am reminded of this even more as Christmas approaches. People are showcasing the gifts they have got their kids on social media. They share huge Christmas Eve boxes, which are beautifully made, and which show heartfelt creativity at times. But the problem that comes of this is that the image reaches someone who doesn't have the funds to create something similar and it produces a sense of obligation and failure in that person. Our photos are far-reaching once we put them online and you never know whose pain it might stir up. But at the same time, you can't bend over backwards in every one of your actions to avoid that. You can only put your positivity out with good will and hope that it inspires somebody.

This is the danger of comparison and giving ourselves reason to strive. I never find that I create the best when I'm running to reach a goal or whenever I'm driving myself to make as much as I can. It takes the joy out of the whole thing because I'm rushing and trying too hard. Most people find themselves happiest in the moments when they let go and just see what happens. I don't know why our society is so success driven, but it's unhealthy and no other era has pushed this in the same sort of way.

This reminds me of our society's attitude to work too. Decades or centuries ago, it was ok to be settled in a low paid job. Now, if you want to work in a restaurant or a shop, it's considered a stop off on the way to success. People use it as a way to fund themselves while they're striving in another area. And there is nothing wrong with that if that's what you truly desire. But it's ok to spend your days pouring coffee for people or serving lunches or helping to pack bags of groceries. I don't know why these jobs aren't considered essential or important anymore. Imagine a world without those things in it. It would be a much more difficult and sadder place to be. The jobs that aren't celebrated are often the most important and the things we take for granted. I think we need to take apart this hierarchy that has been created and realise it's just a construction made by human insecurity and a system of control we have fallen prey to. The same can be applied to the way in which we create. There is no need to strive. We can be creative in whatever ways we like. We don't have to achieve something great. It's important to cover the "small" things too. They are just as needed as the big designs.

Our creativity is worthy, whatever form it comes in. It doesn't have to be "perfect" enough to be featured on the front page of a magazine and it doesn't have to be something huge that changes our entire landscape. I think the best way to enjoy creativity is to just allow it to be whatever it wants and to find the joy in doing it without allowing it to be tainted by strife.

Chapter Twenty-Four - It doesn't Have to be Your "Thing"

As I briefly mentioned earlier, I have a friend who invited me to attend calligraphy classes with her. We went for a number of weeks, and it was a lovely, welcoming environment. We were the youngest people there by between twenty to forty years, but I've always enjoyed spending time with the elderly anyway. They have such wisdom and insight to share over tea and biscuits (which someone kindly made a point of bringing each week.) The class was held in an unheated room in a church. (This was before the cost-of-living crisis but clearly, they had some sort of godly insight into what was coming. That, or their boiler was broken.) We sat with our coats on, scribing with fountain pens. The lady that ran the class was kind enough to supply us with a pen, different sized snibs and a pot of ink. Another lady kindly presented my friend and me with our first calligraphy books. It was traditional calligraphy, so it was very much "by the book." But the lady that ran it was very creative too. I remember she held one class about Christmas cards and envelope designs. She showed methods of incorporating calligraphy into watercolour paintings to make personal cards and envelopes to post to friends and family. She wasn't thinking of selling anything; she was just doing it for the sheer enjoyment of it. My friend and I were both doing fine with calligraphy. It reminded me a little of writing out music in school, keeping everything neatly within the stave and never straying too far from the formula. We ended up stopping going because the classes were called off due to Covid. We didn't go back once they resumed. I guess it just didn't fit in with our new routines, or we didn't feel called to do it. It doesn't mean I didn't enjoy it. I've even held on to the calligraphy materials in case I ever decide to return to it.

Anyway, I was asking my friend what she thought of it after the classes, and she said she enjoyed it, but she wasn't sure if it was her "thing." I felt the same way about it. I might have been good at it, and I might have enjoyed it but that didn't mean it was my life's calling. But that doesn't mean I can't do it. I might go back to it at some stage when I have a bit of extra free time, or maybe I will just do some of it at home with the materials I already have. It might not feel like something clicked when I started it, like it did with writing. And you don't have to ever "click" with something to have permission to do it. You should just try things and do them anyway. Even things that don't lead to a job or a passionate hobby are still good uses of time. You can dip into something and then leave it for a while. There are no creativity police that are going to come after you to see why you haven't settled on something or finished your projects.

My friend and I had a long conversation about crafting and finding your "thing." She felt like she hadn't found hers yet. Maybe she just hadn't found something she enjoyed enough yet to repeatedly do it. But one creative task leads to another, and it all brings goodness into your life. I enjoyed spending time with my friend doing something quiet and chatting with some of the ladies at the class. There was something soothing about making dramatic, inky sweeps on a page and dipping the snib in the ink pot. It was a bit like how I feel whenever my kids and I visit the folk museum and we are transported back in time to a simpler way of living. It makes you put your phone away and use your hands and your ideas.

We talked about so many different crafts after that; my friend even thought about learning more about paper quilling. Going to one class opened up the door to a lot of creative discussion and the possibility of trying anything we wanted. For that reason alone, it was a good use of time.

Chapter Twenty-Five – Being a Beginner

You mightn't identify as "creative" or a "crafter." I never considered myself to be either of those things, but I still make things and play around with ideas. If you walk into one of those huge craft shops, it can be overwhelming, even when you know what you're there for. There is such a volume of materials and if you don't know about the project you might take up, you get daunted and don't know where to start. You don't have to know what you're doing to be there. You can just peruse the shelves and see what you find. I've always felt daunted by entering hardware shops. I don't know what half the tools are for, but you don't have to have an education in woodwork to gain entry to the shop. I see so many people writing themselves off as not creative enough to set foot in a craft shop or to do a craft with their kids. Maybe they don't want to experiment with that kind of creativity, and that is fine too. There shouldn't be any pressure. We should be allowed to have a look around and to window shop for a while. We can try something, decide we don't enjoy it and abandon it midway. There is too much pressure to always be making the most out of every moment – and by that, I don't mean enjoying ourselves – I mean squeezing as much productivity out of every moment as we can.

Over-achievers are a certain breed of people that I don't fully identify with. I guess they were just born with an inbuilt need to succeed or to prove themselves, or they came from families where they always had to impress someone. Whenever we come across them in the creative sphere, it can make us feel like we are treading on someone's toes by even sticking our heads in to take a look around. You don't have to be an artist to have a look in an art supplies shop.

I remember going to an art shop in Glasgow. Even though I had been into other craft and art shops before, I felt a bit lost and overwhelmed in it. I'd been given a list of supplies I had to buy before starting the art class. It involved materials I hadn't used before – like charcoal, graphite pencils, palette knives. I was intrigued by it all, but I didn't know what half of it was for or how to find it. It turned out the teacher of the class had already arranged for the shop to put together a set box of supplies that you could buy for the class. But once I got there, I realised it wasn't so daunting after all. It was interesting looking around and I took the time to have a browse and find out more about what the different materials were.

Sometimes, we dread doing things because we worry we don't know enough about them. But if we never start, we'll never learn. Every expert on something started as a beginner. Our perception of something is more important than the thing itself. I realised this as I was watching my daughter completing a drawing for school. She had to copy an illustration from a book. I've always thought she was naturally great at drawing. I could see she was artistic as soon as she picked up a pencil, but she always notices the parts that she doesn't like. She ended up feverishly rubbing out part of the picture and redoing it several times until she'd decided it was perfect. I thought it was perfect the first time, but she didn't want to hear that. She reminded me so much of myself in that moment, and I felt sorry for her – that she had inherited that harsh inner critic. She seems to jump to critiquing her work rather than celebrating it and that's the curse of being a perfectionist. I haven't taught her to be like that, so I guess it must be a genetic thing (one I wish I hadn't passed on to her.)

But watching her made me realise, maybe it wasn't that I wasn't naturally good at drawing – but I just never believed that I was. I always thought that everyone else knew more than me, so there was no point in trying to catch up. There have been so many times that I have walked into an artistic sphere, and I've felt like an imposter, even though I was probably practising art as much as any other artist there. Our perception of something can make or break it for us. Even if you have a strong negative inner voice, I think it's important to constantly challenge it and do battle with it – otherwise, it deprives us of many great opportunities, all because it has persuaded us of its lie.

Maybe the thing you were too scared to try will end up being the thing you love the most. You don't always naturally uncover your greatest gift by the age of five. Maybe you never got the opportunity to do it at that age, or you didn't have the materials, or your parents didn't enjoy that particular activity. I think it's important to allow yourself to explore it, if you feel the drive to do so. You can keep moving through the self-doubt and through the impostor syndrome when you're standing in an art shop, scanning the shelves, unsure of what to buy or where to even start looking. And it's always ok to ask.

I remember when I went to buy my first drum kit. I didn't have a clue what I was doing. I didn't know which one to buy or what to ask; but I wanted to learn drums, so I overcame that fear. Sometimes, you just have to walk in somewhere before you've had time to talk yourself out of it. When it comes to stuff like that – sometimes it's better to act first and think later. I ended up being greeted by a very friendly, helpful guy who basically made all the decisions for me. He even provided me with a DVD that showed you how to assemble your drum kit. I didn't bother with that though – I've always been too impatient to read instructions manuals or to sit the whole way through an instructions DVD. I did try to do it when I got a sewing machine, but that was because I knew I'd be sitting there until next century trying to work out how to sew a zip on.

The point is, even though the whole thing was overwhelming and intimidating, I got through it, and I did learn how to do it. I just had to take my time and figure it out as I went along. Once I got into a band, I had to dismantle and reassemble my kit constantly anyway. The more you do it, the quicker you get at it. And I was doing it without the basics in a way – they had never provided me with a drum key. On the day I bought the kit, I didn't know what that was, but it turns out it was pretty important. Still, I managed to improvise with tools from my dad's toolkit, so I got by without it. You always get there in the end, if you're determined enough to keep trying and to learn past the stage when you "suck."

Everybody has a moment when they feel like flinging their drumsticks out the window, or maybe even the bass drum. I have thrown pictures away that I truly hated, even after spending hours or days completing them. It's discouraging, but it doesn't have to be the thing that stops you. Even if your painting ends up a crumpled mess in the recycling bin, it has still taught you something you needed to learn. I no longer see these moments of "failure" as failings in me. I used to take them deeply personally and use it as evidence against myself that I couldn't do whatever I was trying to master. But I still had the drive to keep going, and even if I threw it away in that moment, there was always a moment when I wanted to come back and start over later. I still do it now. There is never a stage you reach where you stop making mistakes. I threw a painting out last week. I might do them more often now, but that doesn't mean that I'm always happy with what I'm doing. If it's something I can bear to look at, I keep it, even if I don't love it now. You never know what might end up happening later, or what you might think with the distance of a few days.

Chapter Twenty-Six - Creativity is Play

Creativity is made into something far more serious than it should be. I think that's what happens when you get older – everything gets more serious than it needs to be. Being creative is just playing. It's meant to be fun. If it isn't fun, don't do it. You might just be working on the wrong thing. If you're overthinking it, take a break from it for a while. I have broken writer's block so many times before just by doing that before. Sometimes stepping away from a project is the last thing you want to do. You might feel like you've become so invested in it that's it's hard to take a step back. Or maybe you're just sick of looking at it and you want it to be over – and that's the point at which you definitely need to step away. Relinquishing control can be hard, but if you lose that playfulness that makes art flow, you're lost anyway.

Being creative should always feel like fun. Sometimes you might have time constraints placed on you because it's for work or there is some sort of deadline looming. But that doesn't mean you have to hate every moment of it. It's fine to take breaks from something, or to ask for extra time in which to complete it. You can't always set a timer on creativity. It's different if you're writing a report or something, but if you're waiting for the muse to step in, sometimes you can't force that stuff – especially when you're doing it for the pure pleasure of it.

I've been guilty in the past of taking things too seriously when they didn't need to be treated that way. For example, I might have decided I wanted to make a gift for a friend, but when I started to make it, it didn't look at all how I wanted it to. Instead of allowing it to become something else, or just enjoying the process of making it, I'd allow that self-hatred to take hold. I'd start internally blaming myself for it all going wrong and I'd direct that loathing into whatever I was making too. A gift definitely shouldn't be given in that way. If you're hating every minute of doing something and you aren't happy with the outcome, why are you doing it? Is it obligatory? Or is it something you have pushed yourself to do? These days, more often than not, I create art for no reason. If I end up publishing or releasing something, that's a happy benefit – but the enjoyment should come first. Creativity just isn't the same as working in an office job. You can't hit targets on the clock. It's something that grows and evolves on its own and you can't guarantee perfection by five o'clock. If you need extra time, it's better to allow for that and to factor it in before you start than to put that type of pressure on yourself. Some people perform well under pressure. I always felt like I did in school, but when it comes to art, it's a little different than that.

Being creative is just part of being alive. People do it without even giving themselves credit for it. We are using creativity in everything we do – in every idea that we come up with. I think it has just become contaminated by things like art courses and officious recognition of "successful" artists. Although those things have their merits, it can affect our definition of creativity when we hyper-focus on them. Art doesn't have to be worthy of an award to count as art and we all have permission to create it. Playing should never stop being fun. That doesn't mean you have to enjoy playing make believe with your kids' playsets, but you can play in a million different ways. You're playing when you get out a board game, you're playing when you draw doodles in a notebook, or when you create a cinema night at home, or when you have a long bath and let your ideas dance around in your head. It's whenever you entertain the fun part of your personality that you were taught to suppress in childhood, or once you'd outgrown it, at least.

Making people laugh is creative, gardening is creative, baking bread is creative, writing letters is creative, walking a new route and daydreaming is creative. The list in inexhaustive and no one gets to decide what creativity does or doesn't look like for you. It just means you're in a light-hearted mood, playing around with ideas, trying new things or giving yourself the permission to do whatever you consider to be fun. Why should anyone be able to put limits on that for you, because of their limited definition of what creativity is? Creativity is everywhere and in everything. You just have to stop and look around to see it.

Chapter Twenty-Seven - Ideas to get your Creativity Flowing

Everyone gets stuck for ideas sometimes. Sometimes, I convince myself that I've entirely lost my ability to create. Sometimes, it helps to read ideas, even if you have no intention of practising the specific ones listed. It just unblocks something and helps to open your mind to creative playfulness. I bought a book a long time ago called "1000 Ways to be Creative." If you asked me how many of the exercises I have actually completed, my answer would probably be a big round zero, but it has often sparked something in me that led me to create something else. So, I thought I would share some ideas I have that help me to get creatively unblocked. When you're stuck on something, or stuck with getting started at all, it can be helpful to shift your focus to a different area. Then, when you return to your original idea, you're looking at it with fresh eyes instead of tired, heavy ones.

Make some iced cookies. Go overboard with sprinkles. Get all your supplies from the pound shop and make the happiest looking cookies you can make.

Go for a long walk somewhere that you find inspiring. If you live in an area that resembles an industrial estate, get out of the grey concrete and into a different zone. You can hop on a bus and go somewhere unplanned, you can go to a forest or to the seaside or you can pick a local street that has beautiful nature in it. Note whatever thoughts come to you as you're walking, or just take the time to notice everything that is happening around you. Sometimes it even provides inspiration for stories. If you witness something interesting happening, it might act as a prompt for you.

Go stargazing at night. Wrap up warm and bring hot chocolate. If it's too cold, sit in the car and look through the windscreen whilst listening to calming music. Let your thoughts meander.

Get watercolour pencils and draw on the windows (it can be removed with cleaning spray and a cloth when they start to wear off.) You'll get to draw and look at the view on the other side of the window at the same time. I did this before and noticed so many birds coming and going while I was doing it.

Get a day ticket for the bus and go on as many different buses as you like to areas that you never explore. Look around in their charity shops and see what you find. Try to uncover new parks, new coffee shops and architecture/landmarks.

Go on a coffee crawl. Only have coffee in places you ordinarily never visit. Break your routine and shake things up. Bring a journal or a sketchpad with you. I saw a girl painting with watercolours in a café a few months ago and it was lovely to see someone doing something other than staring at their phone or computer. I do this with journals, write my books on paper to get a screentime break or I write gratitude entries too. You could also choose at seat at the window and just people watch while you enjoy your coffee.

Go for a cinema visit. If you can, go by yourself. Treat yourself to popcorn and a drink. Pick something you don't usually get time to watch and enjoy spending time by yourself. I love going to the cinema alone; it's one of my favourite things to do on the rare occasion my kids aren't with me.

Go to an event you wouldn't usually think of, like a music performance, go to see the orchestra, go to a carol service or look out for street theatre. Look up all the free events in your area and put them in your planner now so you don't forget to go to them. Do something different as a treat. Go to a wine-tasting event, a walking tour or a reading group in the library. Check out local community centres to see if they have any events on too.

Make your own bookmarks. This is a simple craft, and you can do whatever you like with it. You could use fabric, or card or scraps you were planning on throwing away. Add ribbon, lettering, glitter pen, patterned paper, collage, sketches, cartoons, quotes. Make lots of different ones and give them to family and friends as presents. I always need a bookmark and never seem to have one, so I think we should bring them back.

Plan ahead for parties and make lists of ideas. There is always so much to prepare for a party, so make it easier on yourself by thinking ahead while your head is clear. I try to stock up on wrapping materials I come across throughout the year. It helps you to think resourcefully and to be more creative in your recycling. Sometimes, you will receive something that arrives in lovely paper that can be reused. You can build a party cupboard filled with supplies or presents you come across in charity shops. It's easy to find new items that have never been used and you will be glad of the supply you have built up when a birthday or Christmas rolls around.

Make paper crafts like you did when you were a kid. Make paper snowflakes or origami or chains of paper people. Decorate your walls with them to cheer up your home. Sometimes having childlike artwork around your house lifts your mood and gets you into a playful and creative mindset.

Make art out of things you already have lying around in your house. You can even make your own supplies. I made crayons with my kids before. We just used lots of broken crayons and put them in muffin cases, baked them in the oven until they melted and then let them cool and set. It produces swirl effect crayons and the kids loved colouring with them afterwards. (Just don't use a tin you really care about – or reserve it for this – ours got permanently stained!)

Clear out your wardrobe and organise it in a way that encourages you to be more experimental with your clothes. Most of us reach for the same items over and over, but if you shift it all around, you will be able to see the neglected items when you open the door. Donate things you don't use. When my mental space is feeling cluttered, it helps to declutter my physical space. Sometimes everything in life feels disorganised and you don't know what to start with first. But if you clear the surfaces, you can more clearly see what's important and what you want to do in that moment. The same can apply to craft supplies. I like to keep what I know I'm going to use. We can get crowded with ideas and things sometimes, and if you clear out what you aren't going to do and get honest with yourself, it makes it easier to see what you do want to spend time doing.

Go on a mini break. Even if you don't want to book an Airbnb or a hotel, you can still take a day trip. Get a train to somewhere you never go to and enjoy the journey. Whenever everything was getting a bit stifling for me when I lived in Glasgow, I used to jump on the train to Edinburgh. It's only a fifty-minute train ride, but the energy there is completely different. Sometimes you just need to look at different scenery and strangers' faces for a change. See how it changes your feelings when you return home. Do you feel refreshed and more able to focus? Sometimes I think we just get bored and everything around us feels stale and we need to shake it all up and make it interesting again.

Make postcards for your friends or family. You could draw your own pictures or make a collage out of magazine clippings. Post them in person for an added personal touch. You might find inspiration to do something else whilst in the process of slowing down and making handwritten cards. You might even receive a reply and start a new tradition.

Create a seasonal corner. It doesn't have to be Christmas or Halloween to decorate. You can make Spring and Summer displays too. Just get pastel or bright colours, add a different colour of fairy lights, decorate with fake or real flowers and knickknacks. You can look out for objects in charity shops if you like, or just pick up one thing a year to add to it. I often make little displays like this, and it really cheers up our home. It also feels like you're marking each season as something new and exciting, which leads to more productivity and creativity.

Use fabric scraps or clothes you are giving away to make your own bunting or patchwork covers, or little gift bags. You can start small if you've never sewn before. My daughter and I both learned to sew just from trial and error. It doesn't matter if you haven't been properly instructed on it. It's a calming practice and you can make it up as you go along if you like. If it's just for you, why does it need to be perfect?

Make your home smell nice. I find that sensory experiences really affect the way I create. For example, if I'm sitting in a really messy kitchen, looking at a pile of dishes and stacks of laundry all around me, it's harder to think about being productive. Whenever my house is really messy, but I want to get stuck in to writing or painting before I get round to cleaning, I change the feel of the place with some jazz, a candle lit beside me, some fairy lights and nice smells. You can buy some appealing candles, wax melts or air fresheners and use those. You can also use cooking to scent your home. There is nothing more comforting than the scent of baking something like cinnamon raisin bread or cooking a pot of cordial on the cooker. You can even just throw some cinnamon sticks in a pot of water and let it scent your house. If the senses are stimulated, or soothed, you're more likely to feel inspired.

I find water hugely soothing. I don't know if it's because I'm a water sign, or if it's just something that most people experience. I love going swimming, soaking in a hot bath or listening to the sound of a water fountain. I just find it calming having it nearby. Watching water moving or listening to the sound of heavy rain makes me feel inspired to create. My mum has a water feature and for a while, she had it in their summer house in the back garden. I remember one day when I was very stressed, she told me to just sit in the summer house and listen to the water running. It's not something we really make time for anymore – just sitting. At first, it feels unnatural after coming from being overstimulated and constantly looking for something to fill your time. But just sitting in quiet contemplation beside trickling water is so helpful to the creative process. Try writing beside a stream or going for a swim or paddle to see what thoughts arise as you do it.

Write some poetry. There are so many different kinds that you will find something to suit you. You could write an acrostic poem, a sonnet, or a simple contemporary piece. Practise reading it out like you would if you were at a spoken word event. You might even decide to share it with real listeners or readers. Sometimes I don't know what I'm going to write, and I don't intend to write anything concrete, but once you put pen to paper, it just comes to the surface.

Pick a different genre of book than you would typically read and make a point of finishing it. Take notes as you go if you like. Some people like to do this, to remember ideas and concepts. It might even provide ideas for your own projects. Sometimes, it's easy to get stuck in a rut, or to just get engrossed by a topic that interests us. But if we look outside that and try something new, we might learn something different. I was recently considering reading one of those twee Christmas stories I see peppered all over the library, just to prove myself wrong about them being trashy and to see if it informs my writing in any way. Everyone has their own style in whatever they make, and sometimes deviating from that and exploring something new and uncomfortable can inspire us in ways we couldn't have imagined.

Bring plants into your home. I have never been good at keeping mine alive. I just don't seem to have a natural talent for it. The plants that thrive most in my house are the plastic kind. But I still try to do it. I recently got a peace lily and I feel like it almost has a calming presence in the house. There is something about being surrounded by greenery and living things that makes you feel more creatively energised. It's akin to walking in a forest and absorbing the good that nature has to offer you. I also just associate plants with good memories. Did you do any gardening in your childhood? Did you ever go to a pick your own farm? Did you plant anything with a parent or grandparent? Do you have good memories associated with a garden or park? It can bring up many thoughts and feelings that you have forgotten about and inform your art.

Go for a walk around a local museum and see what exhibitions they have on. Take the time to read descriptions you normally just walk straight past. See if they have any art events on. Our local museum has a drop-in art room, and they usually always have something creative happening there. See if they have added any temporary exhibitions. I really like looking around the photography ones. They give you so many ideas, not necessarily related to photography.

Make a nature area in your garden. I would never have thought to do this before having kids, but I love doing it now. I'm still not a gardener, but I enjoy setting up little feeding areas for the birds, we made a pond out of a washing up basin and it's easy to make a simple bug hotel. My daughter's school once sent us instructions for making one out of a kitchen roll tube filled with twigs and hung up with string. There is something about providing habitations for nature that feeds the creative process. It's such a mindful thing to do and you get a lot of satisfaction from having birds and wildlife visiting your garden. Even if you don't have a garden, you can make a windowsill garden.

Make s'mores in the garden, or over a baking tray with some tealights in your kitchen. Get some biscuits, candles, marshmallows and chocolate and make toasted marshmallow sandwiches. If you can do it under the stars, even better. I love sitting in the garden when the weather is warmer. You can put out some tealights and get a glass of wine and a blanket to sit on, or in Winter, you can bundle up and take some mulled wine, tea or hot chocolate with you. Just sitting, being, and not doing anything else brings up so many surprising ideas.

Go for a hike or go camping if you have the supplies. I don't know that I'd be equipped to survive proper camping, but you can still experience elements of it during the day. Go to somewhere remote (as long as you feel safe there.) Spend a day eating outside, have a barbecue or go on a walking trail. Doing simple things like that help you to get out of your head. That is the most important key to creativity, I think.

This reminds me of an important point. When I was in a band, I remember the guitarist telling me I was a good drummer, but the only thing I did wrong was thinking too much. Every single time I started thinking about what I was doing instead of just feeling it, I messed up. Even if I didn't make an obvious mistake, I'd just lose the smooth flow of playing. It's the same with dancing. I remember Michael Jackson being interviewed about dancing and he said that the worst thing you can do is think. If you let your brain start interfering with art and music, it tries to make it logical and it removes the instinctual feel of it. That's the thing that I think is most important in creativity. If you don't have that, the art you're creating loses its soul and its individuality. If you pick any artist and look at their work, it doesn't matter how "technically" correct they are if they aren't soulful about it. I used to know someone who played the guitar. He was amazingly quick at running through scales. I remember him using it as his party piece and impressing everyone with his speedy fingers. But it felt like something was lacking, and it took me a long time to work out what it was. He was so focussed on the theory and getting it "right" that there was no personality to his playing. It was like he was just in a race against himself to play as quickly as he possibly could. He lost his tunefulness and the feeling the music needed to have, even though he was technically talented. It's like whenever you go to a fancy restaurant, and you get a perfectly plated up meal. It's usually more of a morsel than a meal and it's all very artfully presented, but I usually find that those sorts of meals are unsatisfying and flavourless. It's like the chef has been so focused on the presentation and impressing people that they've forgotten to put their heart into what they're making. Everything creative should be made with love, not with technical precision. I just think that too much of it spoils art – whatever form it comes in. That's the stuff that belongs in engineering and the world of mathematics. It's a different sphere, even though the two cross over and help each other. One requires perfection, while the other requires heart.

If you really resonate with a piece of art or with a piece of music, stop and ask yourself – what is it about it that you love so much? It will probably never be that it's overly complicated. It will be something simple – like a catchy melody, a feel to the paint strokes, a truth that speaks to you. It is rarely because you are impressed by the precision of it. You might feel impressed by something like that, but rarely touched by it. One appeals to your appreciation of skill; the other speaks to your soul.

It's true that you do need a certain amount of skill in something to do it well. You can't jump into calligraphy without knowing any of the pen strokes, you can't play a piece on the piano without knowing any of the notes, but if you micromanage those aspects, you lose something essential to art. It's the same, whether you are composing a musical masterpiece or you're making your own jam or making cards for your friends. If you focus on whatever you perceive to be "wrong" or not accurate enough, it doesn't just spoil what you're making, but it ruins the experience for you too. Creativity should always be fun. Whenever it stops being fun and starts being stressful, that's a signal that it's time to take a big step back from what you're doing, or to do something else for a while.

Chapter Twenty-Eight - Multiple Projects

I never used to understand people that read multiple books at the same time. I have recently started to do that myself, but when I do, I usually find that I don't make any headway until I settle on one. I don't think that's necessarily how it works with creative projects. Sometimes, I'll stop and focus on one thing and get it finished – usually because it's been nagging at me, or I feel a huge passion to get it done. At those times, I don't interrupt the flow by starting something else. But there are other times when I find working on different things at the same time helps to unblock me ideas-wise. Sometimes I'll get frustrated with a book I'm working on, so I'll do something fun instead. This week, I was feeling overwhelmed, so I made my own Christmas crackers for myself and the girls. Since they are just for us, there is absolutely no pressure to produce works of art, and it was an opportunity to just play. I made them up as I went along and put whatever I could fit inside them. It has nothing to do with writing and it didn't directly help my writing process at the time. But in the end, it turned out it did help. Here I am, writing about it in my book, but it also created a diversion that got my thoughts freely flowing again and it brought me back to my writing, refreshed. When you're feeling disenchanted by something, you're never going to do it well. Sometimes that just comes from staring at something too much. It's like whenever you can't see the mistakes when you're editing your own work. My friend does some editing and she told me the problem is that as a writer, sometimes you can't see the wood for the trees. I think that's a good way to describe it. You get so bogged down in it that you can't see the bigger picture and then you end up missing the smaller details too. You can't expect to create something great when you've sickened yourself with it. You could apply that to anything. Think of the number of people that are stuck in jobs that bore them and they don't progress in them and just stay, performing at the same mediocre level. They aren't inspired to try harder or to do anything differently, so they don't. They're just sitting at the same screen and the same job day in, day out. It's the same when you turn a project into a chore. There have been times when I've been desperate to finish a story, just to get it out and to move on to something else, but I had lost the passion to write it well. You can plough through that project, keep going and get it finished, but will it produce something you're happy with? It's better to take a break and to do something different than to perform at a lesser level than you're capable of.

I often find that creativity is like a kid that wants to play with you. Once you turn it into a job, they don't want to play with you anymore. It's like they can sense that you aren't doing it with the right spirit and it's no longer heartfelt. Finding a side project or just playing around with a different idea is like providing the kid with a new toy. It gets you started with playing a new game and then you end up coming back to the old one again and it's no longer boring. Sometimes, it takes you on an entirely different path and you don't come back to the original project for a long time again, but you get engrossed in something else. There have been times when I have started a book, abandoned it, and finished another one. I'm still being creative, but it just isn't in the area in which I had originally attended. It's ok to move on to something else if what you're doing isn't working for you or bringing you enjoyment. Even if it's a job, it should still bring you some level of satisfaction. Otherwise, what's the point?

We do so much in life out of a sense of obligation, and there are some things that are unavoidable, whether we want to do them or not. But creative play shouldn't be one of those things. Even if I have something I'm determined to finish, but that I'm not particularly enjoying, I try to have a side project going that I'm truly enjoying and that helps me unwind and feel lighter hearted about being creative again. Each time I find myself struggling to be creative, it's usually because I've lost that light heartedness.

The questions you regularly need to ask yourself as a creative:

Am I enjoying this?

Am I stressed by what I'm making?

Am I taking breaks?

Am I sleeping properly?

Am I driving myself too much?

Do I feel happier when I'm working on this?

Do I still see the purpose in what I'm doing?

If you're truly honest with yourself about these questions, it's a good barometer of where you stand in relation to your creativity. If you feel like the answers are pointing towards a negative outlook, it's time to step back and take a break. You can still be as creative as you like, but it just needs to be directed into a different area for a while.

People often ask me where I get my ideas from. I don't think I have any more ideas than the average person – I just grab onto them as they're passing through. People that think they have no ideas, or that their ideas are bad, or that they aren't creative just aren't tuned in to their creativity – but it is still always there, waiting for them. I have phases where I convince myself that I can't do it – that I can't find ideas or that I can't create. Usually, I find that I'm just not paying attention to my ideas, or that I'm burnt out. You are only human, and you can't create like a machine, and it isn't healthy to do so. The more you let go of controlling your creative process, the more creativity flows to you in abundance. It's like a tap. If it's already turned on, there's nothing else you need to do. If you keep interfering with it, the water won't flow as freely.

Pay attention to whenever you feel your best; that's when you're most aligned with your purpose. If you're doing something and it's making you miserable, it's ok to quit. I think society has trained us to stick with things, even when we hate them. Sometimes, in life, we undeniably have to do that. You can't give up on everything you don't want to do. Sometimes you have to confront fear and jump over the hurdle to grow. But if you're working on something creative and you're not enjoying it and you don't feel like you're getting anything out of it — why are you even doing it?

Sometimes, it's good to stop and journal about how you're spending your time. It helps you to identify the areas in which you are wasting it. I often find that there is a vast difference between what I want to be good at or interested in and what I should actually be doing.

For example, the thought of making sculptures appeals to me. I see other people doing it and I think "maybe I should do that too." Sometimes it's fun to mess around with clay with my kids, but I have never truly enjoyed making sculptures. I find the process incredibly frustrating. The clay doesn't move easily in my hands, I always seem to add too much water to it and the whole kiln process just seems like a lot of work to me. I'm not a patient person, so the thought of having to get to a kiln to get something to set and leaving it in there for hours just feels problematic to me. But here's the thing — I might feel inspired at times to use clay, because I watch an artist working with it and they make it look so easy and enjoyable. That doesn't change the fact that I usually don't find it enjoyable. I get trapped in thinking about where I'm going wrong, and that seems to cause it to go wrong even more. The point of this story is, I could spend hours driving myself crazy over trying to create a clay sculpture — or I could put the time into something else instead. Why make myself miserable trying to be good at something that doesn't come naturally to me? Why not do the things that feel easy instead? Life shouldn't be filled with strife, especially not in the free time we should be spending in rest and enjoyment.

Chapter Twenty-Nine - Myths about creativity

There are so many myths surrounding creativity and what it is. I've been working on breaking them down for myself. I used to always tie creativity to making money. For example, if I made something and it didn't attract sales, I would immediately feel like it wasn't real creativity. In my mind, I'd file it in the bin, just because no one wanted to buy it. But creativity has nothing to do with money, and often, people with creative brains don't specialise in money and marketing. I've had this discussion with an artist friend of mine, and she says she doesn't have this inbuilt skill either. If you think about it, they are two divergent talents, and we shouldn't be hard on ourselves because of that. And just because your art doesn't attract money or praise or excitement, it doesn't make it less creative. There isn't a creative hierarchy of acts of creativity that are "true" and "false" acts of creativity; they are all equally legitimate. Making money isn't what marks something as "creative." On a side note, as I'm writing this, I'm realising how often inverted commas are cropping up and I think it's because there are so many assumptions and labels connected to creativity. It's supposed to be an expression of freedom, but ironically, people attempt to squeeze it into categorised boxes that define what it is. We don't need to buy into this. You can make and make and make, and never earn a penny doing it, and that is still creative. You can make artwork that you never like the outcome of, and that is still creative. You can stand and throw paint at a wall and that is still creative.

If you are someone that practises creativity on a regular basis, or as part of your job, it's important to remember not to burden yourself with too many goals within a set time frame. When I'm writing, I tend to set small goals, like a daily word count, because it does motivate you to keep going and to finish your book. When I don't do this, I find that I procrastinate and abandon projects. If you don't write a little consistently, you lose track of where you are in the story, and it makes it harder to return to it. But I used to take my daily word count far too seriously. I would impose it on myself no matter what was happening in life. If I was sick with the flu or a tummy bug, I'd force myself to write through it. If my kids were off school and they were with me all day long, I'd still try to squeeze out my word count. If I was tired or had a lot going out outside of writing, I'd expect myself to stick to it. There are times whenever your week is naturally busier; life just gets the way, or our humanity gets in the way. For example, if it's a dark November day, you're inundated with work, you have a cold working on you and your kids are demanding a lot of your attention, you don't have to create.

There have been times when I have behaved as if there was a creative dictator standing over me with a cane, and if I didn't get exactly 2000 words on a page that day, I'd be severely punished. I've eased off in the last year. I don't produce as many books as I used to in a matter of months, but I still produce several books a year, or several pieces of art. Taking your foot off the accelerator might slow you down a little, but it keeps you steadier. I'm usually happier with the work I've produced whenever I do slow down. It gives you more time to think about what you're doing, and you don't miss the details.

I love Stephen King's book "On Writing" and I like the fact that he suggests putting a manuscript away in a drawer for six months after finishing your first draft. I never do this, but I want to start doing it. It actually takes a lot of self-control to step away from a project you want to finish but jumping in too quickly can cause problems. There have been times when I have read a manuscript seven times in a row and I have still missed mistakes. I know this can always happen, but it's more likely to happen when you've been staring at something for too long. You start to see what you think you see, rather than seeing what is actually printed in front of you.

I don't know where this personal drive comes from. Perhaps it's from looking around too much at the world we live in. Even if you don't consciously look to compare your productivity, we are constantly presented with a measuring stick by society. It feels like this is the age of achievement. Everyone is always flashing their awards at everyone else. It becomes instilled in us that we have to keep performing well for our efforts to count for anything – and this doesn't just apply to creativity. Even things like homemaking aren't contained in the home anymore. Wherever you look, you're confronted with images of how people are decorating, organising and improving their living quarters. It doesn't feel like it's presented for the sake of inspiration. More often, it feels like there is a competitive edge to these photos and videos. It's an effort on the part of the creator to prove their worthiness. Worthiness isn't defined by productivity. That's something I think my mum has always grasped, but that somehow wasn't translated to me. I think the other half of my family were very driven and goals oriented. It rubs off on you, even if it's only some of the time. You get programmed into thinking that hard work equals worthiness – and not just hard work on its own – hard work with acknowledgement through an agency – whether that is school, university, the head of a company, a political figure, someone respected. This always brings me back to a statement by the artist Shayna Klee: who are these gatekeepers? Why do we need their permission to do what we want to do?"

I think it's wrong in many ways that art has fallen victim to this creative criticism. You can't be "right" or "wrong" as a creative. It isn't an exact science, where there is one acceptable answer, and the others are all off the mark. So, who was it that decided what made art good or bad? People are always talking about how art is a subjective thing. Its merit entirely depends on the taste of the observer. But when this observer has been presented with the scorepad on which to write our result, it stops allowing this subjectivity. Why does one person's word become law?

Chapter Thirty - Crushing Creative Dreams

There's nothing as dangerous to creativity as discouragement. It doesn't matter what form it arrives in; all of it is deadly to our creative instincts. In life in general, I find that our instincts are always right. When you don't follow them, that's where you go wrong. I think it's the same with being creative. You should just go with your gut and not stop to hesitate over the details. The more you polish something, the more it loses its soul. If things are allowed to be imperfect in life and still be beautiful, why can't art be the same?

If you think back to when you were a child, did any criticism really stand out to you? Did it affect your trajectory? Was there a moment when you decided you were "bad" at something you enjoyed? Why is it ok for someone to crush your dreams like that? If there were as many artists in the world as there are dream crushers, think how much richer the world could be.

I know first hand that it only takes one flippant remark to put someone off something they adore. Sometimes we discourage others without even realising we are doing it. We find ourselves repeating the things that were said to us in our most impressionable years. But I think it's important to constantly assess and reassess this. Why is it ok to discourage someone from their dream? Why aren't people entitled to create whatever they want without fear of criticism?

If you think of an art critic, it's a very elitist construction. It was probably created to narrow down the arts. If everyone is participating in them, it makes it harder for people to push their way to the top. If we keep it open and welcoming, people will realise their full abilities and more people will choose to step off the hamster wheel that is how our society runs. I think everything in our society is arranged to keep people as orderly and obedient as possible. It doesn't matter to the dream crushers if they stamp out a dream. Many people gain their sense of power from doing that. It's easier to put someone else's efforts down than it is to put their focus into their own.

Can you think of a time when someone said something to you that put you off what you wanted to do? Can you think of a reason behind it that might have motivated them to do that? Was it because of their own insecurity or fearfulness, rather than because of what you were doing?

It's hard to watch others succeeding sometimes. We have a natural tendency to use it to underline our own failings. If someone else is prolifically producing, it makes us feel like we aren't spending our own time valuably. Or maybe we have dreams that we haven't followed, and we feel envious because we see someone else seeming to get there before us. But each dream is unique. We will always produce something new, because we all have different thought processes and perspectives, so there is no need to feel threatened or undermined by other people's successes.

Chapter Thirty-One - You Always Have Sources

Albert Einstein said, "the secret to creativity is knowing how to hide your sources." Even though we all have original and unique ideas, everything is a mishmash of what came before it. We are like walking encyclopaedias, moving through the world, absorbing what we encounter and shaping it in our own way. I was thinking about this recently. There are very few books that are standalone classics. No matter what you select, you will be able to see a point of reference in it or a style that has influenced it, or a theme stolen from something else. That doesn't undermine the importance of the new creation. Think of how much art we would have been deprived of if artists had thrown away their creations because they bore a likeness to something before that came before them.

If we think of a book like "Cujo," there are elements of it that were probably borrowed from the likes of the Hound of the Baskervilles, or similar literature. That doesn't make it unoriginal – that makes it part of a natural progression that takes place in art.

Who are we to deprive the world of art, just because it might be compared to something that came before it, or because it contains similarities to another piece of work.

I recently visited the Ulster Folk Museum, which is a source of endless inspiration to me. It's a museum of old houses, schools and churches from two hundred years ago and there are always acts of creativity sprinkled throughout the town. The people who work there dress in costume and act the roles of the workers and inhabitants of a town in that era.

Recently, we visited the pharmacy, and there was a lady sitting behind the till making a rag rug. It really spoke to me, just seeing her peacefully working away at something with her hands. It reminded me of whenever I was little, and I saw my granny knitting or crocheting and there were no other modern distractions. I asked the lady that was making the rug if she could explain the process to me. It sounded relatively simple and probably would be one of those crafts that once started, becomes second nature to you and you can just switch off while you're doing it. She showed me her design and I was really impressed by it. She had used scraps of old clothes to make a star pattern on the rug. The image wasn't entirely original; it reminded me of many of the crafts I encountered when I visited Boston twenty years ago. There were plenty of quaint shops there filled with star spangled souvenirs, but that didn't take away from what she was making. Just because I could find a point of comparison, it didn't lessen the effect of her creation. I could still see its inherent value and the originality of her design. I think we should stop setting the bar so high for ourselves in terms of what we make. It doesn't have to be "spectacular" or completely original. We don't have to break through a barrier that marks our creativity as ground-breaking. It's ok to sew quietly in a corner. It's ok to have a room filled with paintings you never want to show anyone, as long as the process of creating them brought you positivity.

Chapter Thirty-Two – It's Never Too Late

There isn't a moment at which it becomes too late to start using your creativity. I think people are often under the false impression that you are either born creative or you aren't. The reasons for which you mightn't start off being creative are endless. You might have lived in a household that didn't celebrate it or practise it. Maybe you had really tidy parents that didn't like the mess that came along with it. Maybe you didn't enjoy the limited array of creative activities offered to you in school.

My mum wasn't often uptight about mess, but she always told me she loathed Play Doh. She hated when it got trampled into the carpet, so I don't remember playing with it at home. I also don't remember painting at home, but we did paper crafts and journalling and musical things. We "cooked" with herbs and grass in the garden, so there was creative freedom to be found there. I had a friend that lived across the road from us. I still remember her Barbie car. It was pink and pristine and probably untouched. It was stored on top of her wardrobe in her beautiful, neat bedroom. Not a thing was out of place. Some people prefer to live like that. Sometimes I envy how simple their lives must be because of it. I still can't do it. Even if I try to emulate it, the façade falls away after a week and I'm back to creative chaos again. I still remember excitedly asking my friend if we could play with her Barbie car. She shook her head sadly and said her mum didn't allow her to play with it in case she made a mess. She wasn't even allowed to get it down from the top of her wardrobe. Even at the age of about seven, it struck me how sad that was and that her mum's obsessive cleaning put a stop to all play. Sometimes we don't grow up in an environment that encourages creativity and play, and that isn't our fault, nor does it mean that the ship has sailed. The ship never sails in terms of our creativity; we can start when we are ninety nine without any experience or background knowledge. Just because limits might be placed on us, it doesn't mean that we have to accept them forever. Think of prisoners that take up arts and crafts behind bars. They couldn't have greater limitations placed on them, but they still find a way. Think of graffiti art. It probably started with someone starved of a chance at creative expression and they let it loose on a blank wall. It has become a respected art form now and people are in awe of the skills displayed by people that were once shunned and accused of property damage. This just goes to show that it doesn't matter if what you create is considered a legitimate art form. Everything that is considered so now was probably once dismissed by someone else.

Just as I tend to gravitate towards chaos and mess, tidier people aren't less capable of creating. Everyone works best in a different environment. Some people, like myself, love background noise. I love having music playing while I work on something, or a YouTube video playing while I paint. I just find myself more focussed under those conditions. I always hated cold, sterile exam halls where all you could hear were the sounds of paper shuffling, teachers' heels and pupils coughing. I'd find the silence anxiety-inducing and I'd always struggle to concentrate through it. Even now, when I'm writing or painting and I notice that something is "off," I usually realise that I've forgotten to put music on or it's just strangely quiet. But I know so many other people that need complete silence to even contemplate working or creating. It's ok to tailor your creative conditions to your specific needs and your personality and no one has the right to tell you that your method is wrong.

Generally, when people criticise your work or your choices or your creativity, it comes from their own insecurity. If something isn't to your personal taste, generally, I find that people don't feel the need to condemn it. They might pass over it or fail to acknowledge it, but they don't feel the need to express strong negativity about it. Who has the right to tell you that what you're doing isn't right or that your process isn't correct?

There is a lot of ageism in our society – and this applies to creativity too. I don't know why our twenties are marked as our most valuable decade and our lives are considered in decline from there. Age and experience develop us and make us richer in knowledge and ideas, so why is aging treated with such contempt? We are always growing, and every year is a gift in which we can learn new things and produce new things. We aren't here to just enjoy flawless skin and a fitter figure. It really annoys me whenever I encounter someone over the age of thirty who believes that they've made their bed and there is no chance to change course. Most people I have spoken to say they're happier at fifty than they were at twenty, with an ill-defined sense of self and a lack of confidence in their choices. Everyone should feel deserving of the opportunity to start something new at a later stage in life. If you didn't consider yourself to be creative as a child, that doesn't mean that you aren't. Perhaps you didn't have the right voices encouraging you then or you just hadn't found an area of creativity you enjoyed. Maybe you were given a bag of pom poms and pipe cleaners and you didn't quite know what to make with them because they simply didn't inspire you. That doesn't mean that you "can't" create.

Chapter Thirty-Three - Inspiration's Mystery

Speaking of inspiration – it is often turned into something elusive and mysterious that the average person can't quite grasp. Self-proclaimed creatives often talk about their muse and where their ideas come from. Perhaps labelling it as such helps creators to classify their ideas as they come in, but there is something elitist about it too. It makes inspiration feel inaccessible unless we are tuned in to some sort off high artistic frequency. I just don't think it has to be that hard. It should be easy and fun, and you shouldn't have to tiptoe around some sort of moody muse, hoping they'll choose to make an appearance that day. If mine doesn't feel like showing up, I go in and drag it out. You don't have to wait for an idea to strike; you can dig around for one until you find it. The process involves more work and it often doesn't feel as magical, but it can still be done. Thomas Edison said that "genius is 1% inspiration and 99% perspiration" and I think this can be applied to creativity in general. You might be lucky enough to have inspiration fall into your lap from the sky, but in the times you don't, if you want to create, its important to just keep going anyway. Sometimes, the last thing I want to do is write, but I just start anyway and see where it goes. Even if I can knock out a 2000-word count without overthinking it, it all adds up to the same grand total in the end, and you can always edit later. Sometimes the most inspired pieces of work you think you've completed look different in the light of a different day. There have been sections of books I have written when I was in a "forcing myself to work" rather than in a naturally creative mode and I was surprised to find they were better than I thought when

I reread them days or weeks later. Sometimes, when we are creating, we can't trust our own filter.

I watched a documentary recently about Sly and the Family Stone. In the documentary, it said that the lead singer began to isolate himself more and more in the studio, layering the tracks with his own instrumentation, rather than using the rest of the band. The producer that was speaking about his process said that the problem with that was that he couldn't assess which work of his was good and which was poor, and he ended up deleting some of the jewels and keeping some of the coals. You can't see what you're doing objectively when you're in the middle of it, so it's important to keep going anyway. You can always edit and cut later, but I think that getting it out there is the most important step to take. If you hesitate and delay working because you're waiting for inspiration to strike or for the right circumstances to present themselves, you'll never create anything.

Another saying of the artist Shayna Klee's that I love is "make bad art and take up space." I completely agree with this. I used to fuss over the details, and I would bin half of what I created because I didn't think it was worthy of taking up space. I would always pick it apart like I was some sort of live-in art critic in my own home. And I wasn't even releasing any of the stuff, so it just became part of a cycle of self-hatred and feeling like nothing I made was ever good enough. As a creator, your job is to create and to try to match whatever vision you have in your head to the one in front of you, but you don't have to dissect it after you've made that. You don't get to decide whether your creation is any good or not. I don't feel like that's for the artist to decide. You don't know what value your creations might have in someone else's life. Maybe they will find exactly what they needed in them, even if you don't. It's impossible to predict the effects of art. If you have the desire to make something, that desire exists for a reason. No one really knows where inspiration comes from or why we feel inspired to work hard on a particular project, but if you have the desire and the ability to carry it through, I think you should. Even if an idea isn't sitting waiting for you, you can still play around and see what you come up with. Not every idea has to be one of genius. But imagine if the genius ideas that have come into existence were dismissed as not being worth chasing down. It's the hard work and discipline of their creator that got them out into the world.

Chapter Thirty-Four - Balance in Everything

I have never been naturally good at doing things in a measured way. I tend to go at something full throttle until I burn out and then I lie like a zombie, barely able to string a cohesive sentence together. Sometimes, when you're in a creative groove and it feels like the ideas are flooding in, you don't want to stop. There have been so many times when I have felt creative, and I have sacrificed sleep and my mental wellbeing to get as much done as I can. I don't think this only applies to creativity; it applies to everything. Our society is such a busy one and everyone is always running around, trying to get as much done with their limited hours per day as they can. But there is always a price to pay for overstretching ourselves. I've been reminded of this in the last couple of weeks. Christmas always becomes like that. We look around and feel compelled to keep up with the pace at which everyone else is living. There are too many options available to us nowadays. Whenever I was little, I don't remember there being a huge number of events scheduled. We attended the odd birthday party or the school nativity or we'd do something simple, like driving around to see the Christmas lights. Now we are over-scheduled. I feel like I'm running a race in which I always finish last, just to keep up with the list of demands from my kids' schools. We get so used to running around all week that I don't know how to stop at the weekend. This year, in the week before the holidays, my kids and I went to a birthday party, a pantomime, a silent disco, a Christmas crackers workshop, a drive-in cinema, swimming lessons and the folk museum. My head was spinning so much from all the activity that I didn't particularly enjoy any individual event. On the day before Christmas Eve, I had booked an elves' workshop for the girls and I to attend, followed by storytelling at the Winter Den in town. It all sounded lovely, but I didn't want to go. The night before, I got a tummy bug, followed by the flu. We spent all of Christmas at home, mostly glued to the sofa, watching films and drinking tea and napping. At the time, it felt like the unluckiest timing possible. I put so much emphasis on Christmas and the celebrations that it felt cruel that on the big day, I couldn't even stomach chocolate. I had spent weeks buying in food and drinks for the week and I didn't have the appetite for any of them. I ended up drinking herbal tea and sleeping through most of the festivities.

In hindsight, this wasn't a bad thing. We were forced to stop running around. My body told me "that's enough" and we were forced into hibernation. We didn't do anything remarkable, and we all watched far too much TV, but it was what we needed. As soon as I got better, my kids got a heavy cold. We are currently still on the sofa. I'm writing on it while we watch a family film, and my kids work their way through their selection boxes. Ordinarily, I'd feel like there is something very wrong about this. I felt guilty the whole time and I felt the pressure to be out and about, doing something "Christmassy." But why do we always have to be doing or achieving something? When I look around at everyone we know, they seem to be doing the same thing. There are perfect photos shared everywhere of all the activities people are engaging in over the holidays and they all look blissfully happy. But we never know the full story behind the pictures. We don't know the thoughts behind the smiles, and things are rarely as simple as they appear to be. When we were having a "great time" and making magical memories, I was hurtling towards burn-out. I might have felt it, but I didn't consciously know it because I was too busy to even pause to consider it.

Anyway, my point in discussing this is that rest is as important to us as activity is. If we don't remember to take it, our bodies force us to take it. I thought that rest was the last thing I needed before Christmas time. I felt like I was behind on multiple projects and I had huge to-do lists in my mind of what I wanted to achieve before the arrival of the new year.

But I didn't get to do any of it, and nothing bad happened. I just found the space and rest that I needed. If you nourish your body and your spirit, you're in a better place to create anyway.

The most restful activity that we did in the run-up to Christmas was our visit to the folk museum. I particularly love going there at that time of the year because it's like experiencing a truly traditional Christmas. All of the plastic tat and the consumer-driven practices have been stripped away and you get to experience something closer to the true meaning of Christmas. It wasn't overly busy and we got to walk around in the fresh air, taking in the festive smells and sights. The girls played with their pretend snow (soap suds) and they made cinnamon toast over an open fire. We were given some roasted chestnuts that had been made outside, there were black and white films playing in the old cinema and we tasted some Christmas fayre. None of it was noisy or over-stimulating, and I could actually feel my creative brain waking up while I was there. We often think that we need constant entertainment and noise to feed our ideas, but it's only when we stop that they start to catch up with us.

There was a moment during which we were standing in front of the fireplace in the church, hearing a gentle recording of carols and looking around at the handmade decorations of holly and spruce tied with string. It helped my head to go quiet in the midst of the craziness, and I realised just how manic the whole season has become (as have our lives in general.)

In comparison to certain people we know, our lives aren't even that hectic, but I still find it all too much at times. I don't understand how some families cope with the fact they have multiple kids' clubs scheduled each day, or the fact both parents are working long hours and juggling childcare. There are so many people I meet that tell me they don't have time to read anymore. If we don't have time to read, how can we have time to think, or create or to reflect on what we're doing?

People often ask me how I find the time to work on different projects. I think being a single parent has helped with this. The fact that I'm in enforced isolation so much means that I have had to come up with my own entertainment. I don't have someone else filling my evenings for me. I find the process of creating restful, so I want to do it, to enable me to unwind. It isn't a chore – most of the time – and when it is, the satisfaction I know comes with a finished project often motivates me to keep creating anyway.

You can be in charge of your creative environment. It's hard in life when we can't control our surroundings. For example, if you work in an office, you probably don't have much say in the chosen décor, the lack of music, the lighting, the ambience, but if you are creating at home, you can choose the surroundings you wish to have. You can choose a gentle environment that makes you feel rested and cosy and primed to create. It doesn't have to feel like work or to feel in any way stressful. There is enough stress that exists outside us in life, without us creating more of it for ourselves in the comfort of our own homes.

When I go chasing after a story, those are the times I end up feeling frustrated. You can run around looking for ideas in the noise. You feel like stories should spring into your busy, over-stimulated mind. But generally, I find that those aren't the times they flood in. It's when we are in a state of repose that we are most receptive to creative ideas.

Our society doesn't encourage quiet or peace. You just have to look around to realise this. I was on a bus earlier today, which isn't a part of my usual routine, but it made me realise how much has changed in the world the last decade. I had a hospital appointment early in the morning, so I was travelling with many people on their way to work. No one around me was looking out the window or staring into space. Every single person was glued to their phone. They didn't even break contact with it when someone got on or off the bus. It felt like everyone had become robotic and they were only existing within the worlds in their phones. I'm guilty of doing this too at times, but I hope I break away from it enough to appreciate a view, to notice things that are happening around me and to have time for the people in the same physical place as me. I know when people are glued to a screen, they could be doing a million useful things. It doesn't mean they are always mindlessly scrolling. They might be doing something creative online, talking to friends, reading a book or one of the other countless tasks we can now do digitally. But it feels like we have been robbed of the present moment and the stillness around us. We aren't allowed to rest our minds. We are conditioned to believe that we should always be doing something "productive." We are constantly accessible, by email as well as by messenger. There is no such thing as down time anymore, unless you make the conscious effort to carve it out. I don't know why having empty hands or an empty mind aren't considered valuable anymore. I've been trying to allow myself to have more of it recently. You need time to check in with yourself and your emotions, to ask yourself questions and to allow ideas to flower in your mind. Just as flowers can't grow without space, ideas can't blossom without the room to allow them to spread out and find their favoured place of anchorage.

There are so many modern conveniences that make our lives easier and quicker. But sometimes, slowing down is exactly what we need to do. For example, in the past, an entire day was devoted to laundry. Everything else was put on the backburner while that task was embarked upon. It sounds arduous and I'm sure that everyone is glad that washboards and mangles are a thing of the past. But it also must have allowed people the time they needed to think things through and to play around with ideas in their minds. It could be a social activity too, but if you think of all the time spent scrubbing and wringing clothes out, there had to be space there to allow your thoughts to freely wander. Our thoughts are constantly being cut short and redirected into something with a definite aim nowadays. We are always reminded that we only have a short number of hours in the day and that we have to fit more into it than we naturally should. It is close to impossible to avoid getting swept up in the tide of over-productivity. We aren't encouraged to rest or to let ourselves not be busy for a while. Sometimes quiet is the thing we need the most – not just creatively, but emotionally. The more I write about creativity, the more I realise its connection to our emotions. One feeds the other and one can't exist without the other. Creativity without emotion feels like a relationship without love and emotion without creativity ends up feeling stifling because there is no release for it. We need to attend to our emotional state first in order to be able to create.

When I was little, we seemed to get power cuts a lot in our village. I always got excited about them coming instead of regarding them as a problem. Granted, we did have an open fire in my first house, a gas cooker and no electric shower, so it wasn't life-stopping when it happened, but it forced us to slow down. Even though the nineties were a slower time in many respects, we were still used to flipping lights on and off without giving it a thought and watching the TV whenever we felt like it. When those options were removed, we had to light candles, have a bath by candlelight, read in front of the fire and listen to silence rather than to tapes or the radio. I liked the enforced slowness of those days. We managed fine by candlelight, and I loved curling up in front of the fire with a book. I can't picture my own kids doing that as easily. They've been born into a rushed world where everything is always "go, go, go!" I find the holidays an excellent opportunity to undo some of this, but it definitely has to be a conscious decision. If a power cut happened now, I think we would struggle much more with it. We tend to have more food in the fridge, our cooker is electric, we rely on the toaster, microwave, Alexa, electric showers. Everything has sped up and become easier, so long as we have the conveniences at our fingertips. But sometimes it is made too easy for us to hurry through our days. When I was little, we didn't have a toaster and making toast under the grill was a slower, more mindful process. You had to keep an eye on it. I can remember my mum making "melba toast" to use up the ends of the loaf. I can't imagine ever taking the time to carve slivers of bread off the heel now. We just don't have time for the same slow things. I think this time of technology has stolen a lot from us. We don't have to take our time doing things, so we race through everything and I feel constantly out of breath because of it. That's why being ill can sometimes be a strange kind of blessing in disguise. It forces you to stop when you normally don't feel like you have permission to do so. That's why I love to book a little cottage beside the sea or somewhere remote during the holidays. I try to find one with an open fire too. When we arrive there, it always feels unnaturally quiet to begin with – almost uncomfortably so. But you soon adapt to the silence and it gives you so much room to think about things – creative projects and every other aspect of your life.

If you don't listen to the signals coming from your body that tell you to slow down, it usually puts a stop to your activity for you. That is something I am still learning. Each time I get sick, I know that I have been run down in the lead up to it. There have always been signals to slow down that I haven't taken because I'm not paying attention to them, or I brush them off as unimportant. But, they always make sure to let me know how important they were when they stop me in my tracks.

I often hear the question "where do you get your ideas from?" I usually brush it off because I still have the tendency to think my ideas are stupid. But somewhere inside me, I must think they have value because I continue to put them out there. I think that question is misleading because it assumes that creativity is something we hunt down or something we consciously choose. Although there is work and commitment involved in creating anything, I don't believe we find ideas; I think they find us. When your mind gets really quiet, that's when they start to come in. So, I don't think whenever people say they don't get ideas that that is the case; I think that either they haven't had the chance to hear them in all the noise we are living with, or they just don't place value on the ideas that do come through. Think about all the ideas you've had that you might have dismissed as silly or pointless. What would have happened if you'd run with the idea instead? You can't judge your own ideas; you get them for a good reason, so why not start listening to them? No bad can come from pursuing an idea but so many regrets come from ignoring them or dismissing and forgetting them.

Chapter Thirty-Five - Not Having Enough Time

This must be the most-used excuse to get out of creativity and I have used it myself. We all have the same number of hours in a day. Yes, some of us have more commitments than others – whether it is a demanding job, family to care for or other obligations, but we still have twenty-four hours to play around with. Maybe we just need to start setting boundaries around our time. Our time is just as valuable as our health or money, but we often don't place value on it. We don't think of time as something we can over-give, but we can. Since being a parent and tuning in to my own limitations and needs, I am really protective of my time. People are often careful about where they direct their money because they can clearly see when the pot is empty but there is no gauge to show us when our time is being over-dispensed. Sometimes, the signs of this are right in front of us and we don't even see them. How many of us have planners that have writing scrawled all over them? I know so many people that have to add post-its and arrows extending their days just to cram it all onto the page. It is a great visual representation of how overstretched we are. When it gets like this, it's important to stop and ask yourself what you can afford to cut. Sometimes you have "obligations" that can be stopped without the world collapsing around us. We are so used to living with so many of these that we don't even question it or stop to wonder if it might be unhealthy or damaging to us.

I always think back to the 1800's whenever I want to slow down. People used to achieve a lot, but they also had so much down time. Women used to sit and sew, conversing with one another or just listening to the thoughts in their heads, but most of us don't have time for this now. I have a pile of clothes to be repaired that I haven't got around to mending yet. Granted, I have one functioning hand at the minute (I broke the other one), so I'll let that one slide, but there are so many things that are neglected because we don't have enough time in our days to do the things. The way we measure success nowadays is completely warped. We think if someone wears themselves into the ground from working so hard they're succeeding. Or people basically prostitute themselves on social media to try and earn the likes and follows of as many strangers as they can. When did this all become normal to us? I know it must have been a gradual process because if you were to interview someone from a century ago about the way we live now, they'd probably think it's crazed. Is the way we're living conducive to creativity though?

I know artists that end up sacrificing their love for their craft by turning it into a successful career. It loses its heart when there is too much pressure put on it. We were never made to live at the rate at which we are expected to now. We don't have adequate time for reflection, or to even question the speed of the world we're living in.

That was one benefit of the pandemic: it forced us to adopt an older style of living. We were confined to our homes for much of it. As someone who is always going out and keeping busy, it was a hard adjustment to make. But once the initial shock of it wore off and we adapted to it, I thought that many positives came from it. My neighbours and I got to know each other better and we shared recipes and baked goods with each other. My kids and I had more time to complete all the things we never got round to doing together. We went for long walks and appreciated nature again, we made art together and learned how to be more patient. (Home-schooling definitely forced me to do that.) In a way, I miss the quietness now. It feels like we are expected to return to the busyness that existed beforehand, but we are different now. You can't go through something so life-altering and then return to the same routines, feeling content about it.

There are so many creative things that people might label as pointless or unproductive, but doing them brings you joy, and one creative act always feeds another, creating a chain of creativity in your life. For example, my next-door neighbour saved the seeds she got from a honeydew melon and she told me about how, as a kid, she dyed them, threaded them and then hung them up, so I decided to try it. It was extremely time consuming. First we had to let them dry out for days, then we had to dye them different colours, then I sat and laboriously threaded each one onto a long piece of thread with a needle. It felt like it took an age, but it was strangely rewarding too. I still have it hanging up in my kitchen as a decoration now. It wasn't the type of craft that you loudly brag about on Instagram and it doesn't look impressive, but it cheers me when I look at it because it reminds me of that simpler time and being creative with my kids. It forced me to slow down and concentrate and I felt that it really benefited my mental health. It was such a simple idea, and it costs nothing to make, but it felt valuable to me. So, you shouldn't dismiss any creativity as being a waste of time. The outcome of it doesn't matter as much as the process itself – which leads me on to the next chapter.

Chapter Thirty-Six - Savouring the Process

As a writer, I tend to jump ahead to the end result of whatever I'm working on. That isn't necessarily a bad thing. It helps you to finish something if you have an aim in mind, however vague, but that isn't the reason you should do it. When I wrote my first book, I was dying to get it out. I thought if I published it that that would be the most important moment to me, but over the years, I have found that it isn't. I get to the point of publication where I'm tying up all the loose ends and I'm sitting up half the night formatting. It's always a frustrating process so part of the joy of publication is just knowing that it's finished – and there's nothing else left to do – until the next book, at least.

Sometimes I've had a mini celebration for a book being published. I open a bottle of prosecco and sit with my feet up, momentarily basking in the glory of having finished a project after months of hard work. But before I've even drained the glass, it hits me that I don't feel as fulfilled as I thought I would. The hunger to write has never been satisfied. As soon as a book leaves my hands and goes out into the world, there is nothing more for me to do to it. That feeling of completion is satisfying for a short moment, but then I realise that life suddenly feels empty. I spent so much time on my book that it probably feels like empty nest syndrome to the parents of recently departed offspring. My brain immediately starts searching for the next book to write. Sometimes I even start it on the same day I've published my most recent one. That's when I realise that the real joy in writing doesn't come from finishing it – it's the process of creating it that brings the most joy. It's strange because, at the same time, it can be incredibly frustrating. Sometimes you just aren't in the right mood to write, and it feels like extracting teeth. Sometimes, you get lost in the plot and you have to scrap parts you've spent hours on. Sometimes, you could cry with frustration at the seeming lack of direction your manuscript is taking. But you always overcome those little writing hurdles and get back into the flow of it. There's something about disappearing into the world you're creating in your head that is empowering and a huge release. It's like going on a holiday in your head. Everything else that's been bothering you is shut off for a while, and that's all you can focus on.

I have always struggled to appreciate pure stillness. I see scenes of people sitting under skies filled with stars, admiring them and appearing to think of little else. I've always found it hard to just be in the moment. While someone else appears to be able to enjoy the simple wonders of nature, I struggle to hold myself on that thought. My mind always wanders elsewhere and I start contemplating our insignificance in the vast universe as we stand under the stars. I end up having some sort of anxiety attack or existential crisis and the moment is spoiled. But writing takes me away from that. I think the fact that you're actively engaged in the creation of a story, both with your mind and your hands means that you're completely absorbed in it and you can't think of anything else. I always return to reality feeling more able to cope after a good writing session. Anything could be happening around me while I'm writing and I'd probably completely miss it. It's my happiest place. I feel the same when I'm painting something too.

Sometimes you finish a project and you are happy with the outcome. More often than not, I'm not. Or if I do like something I've created, it takes me a while to come round to it. You can't appreciate the beauty of anything when you're too close to it. You've been examining its flaws at close range and trying to iron them out, and that's all you can think of when you look at the finished product.

It pains me when I see my daughter putting herself through the same torture I have put myself through for years. She dissects whatever she's making as she goes and ruins the process for herself. She has always loved art and been really good at it, but I think she has stopped enjoying it because of this tendency of hers. Recently, we had a painting session together. I was painting a picture with my left hand for the first time. It didn't turn out well at all. My daughter loved the painting though, so you can never predict what someone else will see in something of yours. In the past, I would have berated myself for how it was turning out and ruined the creative process, but this time, I just enjoyed painting and told myself it didn't matter what it looked like when it was finished. Sometimes, I think it's good to make something that you might even have the intention of binning when its finished. It takes away the pressure and it allows you to just enjoy it. It's like whenever a toddler does fingerpainting. They aren't thinking about how the picture looks or how accurate a representation of a dog it might be; they're thinking "getting myself covered in paint is fun, making a mess is fun." We lose this as adults after being subjected to years or even decades of editorial input from teachers and colleagues and managers. But sometimes, we need to shrug this off and just have fun making something. Who cares what it looks like? And maybe it will end up looking really cool in the end anyway. But if it doesn't, at least you had a good time making it.

This might seem like a bit of a morbid thought, but sometimes I tell myself that everything I've made will be gone one day. A time will come when none of my possessions will exist; they will all have disintegrated or got lost or binned by someone after I'm gone. So, why shouldn't I just enjoy making them? Being creative without worrying about the outcome inspires other people and that keeps the chain of creativity going and spreads the happiness it brings. It's something that carries on through time and generations and it never dies, so that's what is important in life – not how precise your brushstrokes were, or how ground-breaking your song was, or how impressive your piece of writing was. If you impress somebody, that won't be remembered dearly, but if you touch somebody, it will. I think that's the whole meaning in being creative; it's to share ideas, to inspire, to brighten up our lives with art and stories to entertain and uplift people around us. It's to give everyone the chance to be transported to another place when they might be dealing with things that aren't exactly enviable in their current reality. Creativity is what keeps our hope alive when we might have lost everything else that matters to us.

When I was at my lowest point in life and everything was falling apart at once, I didn't know what the meaning of living was anymore. I truly wanted to exit the world and I couldn't find the courage to endure another day, but I started to play around with words and with a paintbrush, just to pass the time. I told myself - if you're forced to stick around longer than you want to, you might as well not be bored while you're doing it. But in doing that, it turns out I found my life's purpose. I just thought I was getting some thoughts down on paper or drawing a picture to keep my hands busy when all I was doing otherwise was chain-smoking and questioning the sky on the need for the continuation of my existence. Making things might sound frivolous, but the process of doing that heals more than anything else I've ever found. The more you tap into your creativity and let go of the fear of failing at it or not being good enough or not having a "natural talent" for it, the more you find your contentment and you remember the fun in life. We can lose that when we get older and develop problems and get bogged down in the serious stuff, but there is always a big kid sitting inside you, waiting for an opportunity to play. We were all born to create in a million different ways, so stop letting the world tell you that you aren't an artist.

Printed in Great Britain
by Amazon

18625734R00078